DAN

The Mal

by Richard Philp

Special Photograph

A Rutledge Book | McGraw-Hill Book Company   New Y

SEUR

e in Ballet

& Mary Whitney

by Herbert Migdoll

Louis | San Francisco | Toronto | London | Mexico | Sydney | Düsseldorf

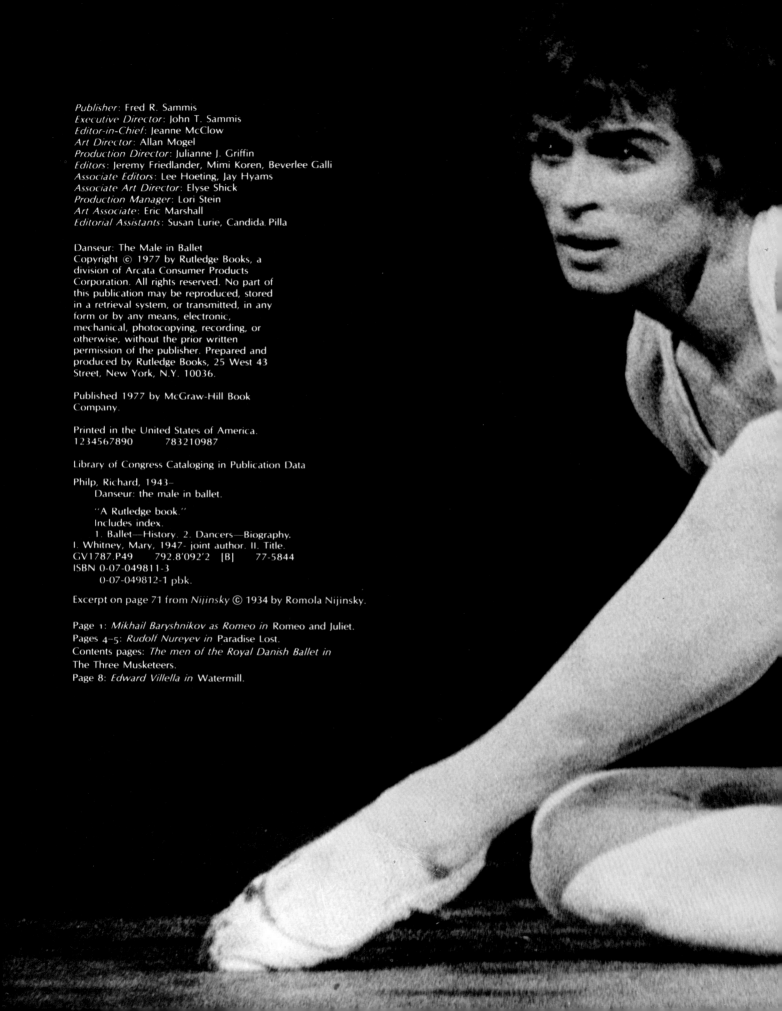

Publisher: Fred R. Sammis
Executive Director: John T. Sammis
Editor-in-Chief: Jeanne McClow
Art Director: Allan Mogel
Production Director: Julianne J. Griffin
Editors: Jeremy Friedlander, Mimi Koren, Beverlee Galli
Associate Editors: Lee Hoeting, Jay Hyams
Associate Art Director: Elyse Shick
Production Manager: Lori Stein
Art Associate: Eric Marshall
Editorial Assistants: Susan Lurie, Candida Pilla

Published 1977 by McGraw-Hill Book
Company.

Printed in the United States of America.
1234567890   783210987

Library of Congress Cataloging in Publication Data

Philp, Richard, 1943–
    Danseur: the male in ballet.

    "A Rutledge book."
    Includes index.
    1. Ballet—History. 2. Dancers—Biography.
I. Whitney, Mary, 1947- joint author. II. Title.
GV1787.P49   792.8'092'2   [B]   77-5844
ISBN 0-07-049811-3
        0-07-049812-1 pbk.

Excerpt on page 71 from *Nijinsky* © 1934 by Romola Nijinsky.

Page 1: *Mikhail Baryshnikov as Romeo in* Romeo and Juliet.
Pages 4–5: *Rudolf Nureyev in* Paradise Lost.
Contents pages: *The men of the Royal Danish Ballet in*
The Three Musketeers.
Page 8: *Edward Villella in* Watermill.

To our parents

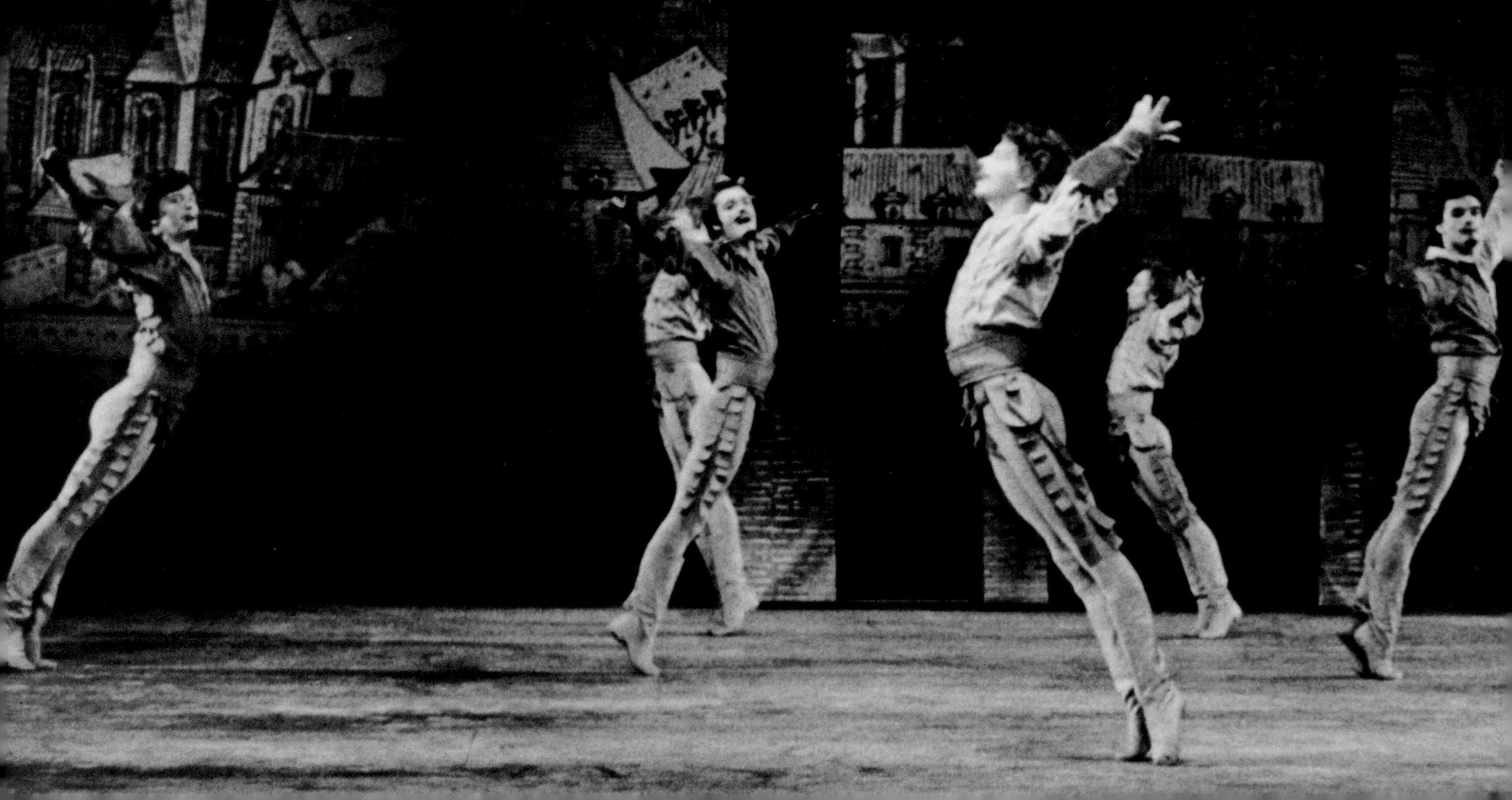

Foreword

The male has always been a prominent element in the world of dance, be it as medicine man, jester, teacher, choreographer, or performing artist.

In ballet, his initial dominance as a performer dwindled, until for many decades of the nineteenth century he was noted more for his teaching or his choreography than for performance; often—and regrettably—the abilities he could display as an artist were overlooked. Certainly during the period of the Romantic ballet, dance was directed toward the beauty of movement created by women. Later on, we find Petipa's ballets still focused on the leading ballerina, such as the Swan Queen in *Swan Lake* or Aurora in *Sleeping Beauty*. But in the early decades of this century, Fokine broke with this tradition by creating exciting choreography for both male and female dancers, allowing each sex to enhance the special characteristics of the other. Instead of limiting the male to his role of gallant partner, ballets were created in which the danseur played a major part: The Rose in *The Specter of the Rose,* the Favorite Slave in *Scheherazade,* the title role and the Blackamoor in *Petrouchka*.

To me, Fokine, the father of modern ballet, set a reforming precedent of male-female equality that has been continued by contemporary choreographers. Although twentieth-century partnerships such as Karsavina and Nijinsky, Markova and Dolin, Danilova and Franklin, Alonso and Youskevitch, Fonteyn and Somes, and Tallchief and Eglevsky were often based on the classics, these dancers also stimulated choreographers to create new works in which the specific talents of both sexes were fulfilled.

It is my feeling that movement can have tremendous sensuality that is not directed to specific sexual gender. Certainly movement for me is totally asexual—both men and women can do any dance step. Of course, some steps have become particularly associated with one sex rather than the other, but I think this is because of some archaic connotations and training habits that still exist in the dance world. We should not forget that Fokine released the male in ballet and enabled him to become a significant performing artist in his own right. As he pointed out, movement must flow from one's emotional responses and should not be tied to the rigidity of classical technique.

It is gratifying to welcome a book that focuses on the varied contributions of men in dance. In tracing the fortunes of the male in ballet, this book reminds us of the significant achievements of great male dancers and choreographers; and in so doing, it reemphasizes the balance between the sexes, which must be maintained in an art form that has its basis in human movement.

ROBERT JOFFREY
Artistic Director
The Joffrey Ballet

Preface

Dance, the liveliest and fastest-growing discipline in the performing arts today, is a tremendously large subject about which surprisingly little of a serious nature has been written. Our investigation involves one principal area of dance: the role played by the male dancer in ballet. Our book is unique in its examination of this important and current topic. But it would be impossible to focus exclusively on the danseur without discussing to some extent the role that women have played in dance and including other significant historical material. Unfortunately, no book of this size, with its generous complement of photographs, could ever begin to convey a full picture of dance history. We regret that many dancers—both male and female—have had to be treated too briefly or even eliminated from the narrative altogether. Our intention, however, was not to write a history of the last five hundred years of ballet's development but, rather, to examine one major aspect of that fascinating history—the danseur. This examination tells us something about current taste, current trends, and ultimately something about ourselves. When ballet has been relegated to the ranks of mere amusement, it has floundered and nearly died; when it has been allowed to express the concerns and moods of the society in which it has been produced, it has responded vigorously, refreshingly, healthily. We are in such a time right now—and the role of the danseur is of vital importance to it.

R. P.
M. W.

1

Aspects
of Men
Dancing

Dance today is the liveliest of all the performing arts. The dance boom, as it has been called, is not confined to our major urban centers; for although New York City has been called the dance capital of the world, an estimated 80 percent of the American dance audience—which numbers about 16 million—is located outside New York. Television programming is beginning to reflect this nationwide interest; the growth and development of well over a hundred regional ballet companies in the past twenty years supports a strong contention that dance is a grass-roots movement; on college campuses across the country, statistics show that dance events can outdraw rock concerts. On Broadway, where companies such as American Ballet Theatre play to sold-out houses, patrons willingly pay as much as $40 for an opening night seat. Although seats to most dance events are well within the means of the average pocketbook, the tickets for a gala performance of Martha Graham's new *Lucifer* in 1975 were priced as high as $10,000 each—and there were buyers willing to pay.

The tremendous growth in the dance audience is a world-wide phenomenon. Within the past few decades, major ballet companies have been established in countries that did not previously have a strong dance tradition—the United States, Great Britain, Germany, the Netherlands, Sweden, Israel, Canada, and Australia, among others. Dancers like Erik Bruhn and Flemming Flindt are national heroes in their native Denmark; Japan is beginning to "export" dancers of international caliber, such as ballerina Yoko Morishita; South Africa has produced a major choreographer in the late John Cranko; and Maurice Béjart's company, Ballet du XXe Siècle (Ballet of the Twentieth Century), based in Belgium, performs all over Europe, and as far afield as Iran, to capacity audiences. But perhaps the most familiar symbol of this international dance activity is the danseur Rudolf Nureyev.

When the Bolshoi Ballet emerged from behind the Iron Curtain for its first visit to the West, in 1956, Russian danseurs astonished European audiences with their unabashed pyrotechnics and virile dramatic power. With his defection from the Soviet Union's Kirov Ballet in 1961, Nureyev quickly became, like the legendary Nijinsky fifty-two years before him, the leading example of what was new and most exciting in the danseur's technique; he set the standards of excellence for all subsequent Western danseurs. Since coming to the West, Nureyev has focused our attention on the most exciting development in dance today: the reemergence of men dancing.

"For us a male dancer is something monstrous and indecent of which we cannot conceive." So wrote Théophile Gautier, the French novelist, poet, and celebrated champion of ballet, over a century ago. Gautier's low opinion of the danseur, far from being unique, reflected the widespread prejudice of the dance-going public of the nineteenth century, a prejudice inherited by many dance lovers of the twentieth.

The male dancer had formerly held an esteemed position, but by Gautier's time, his role had been emasculated, and he was reduced to performing as a *porteur* for the glorified ballerina. His line was expected to be complementary to hers; except on those dwindling occasions when he was allowed to show his own prowess—as a sort of elegant athlete—his demeanor was to be adoring of his lovely, fragile partner, his function to be the unsung hero who made possible her seemingly effortless performance. By the end of the nineteenth century, a stigma was attached to men who dared to make a career of ballet, and it has taken nearly a century for the public to recover its delight in a masculine style of performance.

Particularly within the past decade, we have witnessed a tremendous resurgence of interest in the danseur, in his technique, acting, and roles. It began in 1909, when the great impresario Serge Diaghilev introduced Vaslav Nijinsky to the West—the premiere season of Diaghilev's Ballets Russes, with Nijinsky as premier danseur, took Paris by storm. And it continues today

Preceding pages: *Gregory Huffman, Robert Thomas (center), and members of The Joffrey Ballet in Gerald Arpino's all-male* Olympics. *Opposite: Rudolf Nureyev in Rudi van Dantzig's modern ballet* The Ropes of Time.

Below: *Natalia Makarova in the title role and Mikhail Baryshnikov as her deceitful lover, Count Albrecht, in the nineteenth-century Romantic classic* Giselle. *Right: Baryshnikov and Carla Fracci in John Butler's dramatic pas de deux* Medea, *a work that fuses ballet and modern dance techniques. Opposite left: Modern dancers Merce Cunningham and Cathy Kerr in Cunningham's* RainForest *on the television series "Dance in America." Opposite right: American-born Richard Cragun, a leading dancer of the Stuttgart Ballet, taking class. Few dancers, no matter how great or famous, neglect this daily routine, which keeps their muscles responsive to the unnatural physical demands of ballet.*

in the enormous success of such peripatetic danseurs as Nureyev and Mikhail Baryshnikov, a more recent defector from the Kirov Ballet. The extraordinary talents of these dancers, and their numerous guest appearances with companies around the world, have drawn attention—even adoration—to their art. A danseur like Baryshnikov inspires the devotion of public, management, and choreographers alike, and the name of either Nureyev or Baryshnikov guarantees a sold-out house; it is primarily for these dancers that new works are being created.

In America, the manifest virility of such dancers as Jacques d'Amboise and Edward Villella—who has made public acceptance of the danseur a personal crusade—may also have helped to spark this new, general interest; or perhaps the public glimpses in such stars some of the old charisma of Gene Kelly or Fred Astaire. But probably it has more to do with the rediscovery of the male body as an expressive instrument, both dramatically and musically, in both ballet and modern dance; for it appears that audiences are increasingly intrigued by the wordless, visceral mode of communication that is dance. On a more sensational level, since the standards of virtuosity are so high, sports-conscious America may be responding to the male dancer's energy and dazzling technique.

Though it is becoming a truly popular medium, ballet's

reputation as an elitist art form is well founded. The origins of ballet can be traced to the exclusive circles of European courts, where the initial purpose of the so-called court ballet was to wield political clout, to demonstrate that the reigning monarch was not only rich and powerful but also a person of considerable sophistication; indeed, the royalty of Europe lavished astronomical sums on sumptuous ballet productions.

In the twentieth century, such patronage has disappeared, of course, and in its wake have followed new freedoms and new challenges for ballet companies. On the one hand, experimentation, which was formerly restricted, now has considerable freedom; on the other, ballet companies and choreographers are forced to seek out the largest possible audience in order to survive.

In the process, ballet has rubbed elbows with modern dance, a child of the twentieth century, whose exponents in the early years would have been pleased to wipe away all traces of ballet (the feeling was mutual). In place of ballet's basic positions for the feet and arms, which modern dancers considered unnatural, they substituted such principles as torso contraction and release, or fall and recovery. In the past seventy years, or so, modern dance has developed a myriad of personal styles and methods of expression, unhampered by the rigid move-

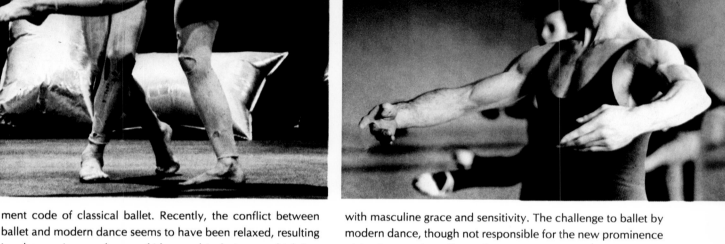

ment code of classical ballet. Recently, the conflict between ballet and modern dance seems to have been relaxed, resulting in a harmonious exchange of ideas and techniques, which has greatly stimulated both forms. Rudolf Nureyev has been a pioneer danseur in this direction, performing not only with the ballet companies with which he is most closely associated, but with the modern dance troupes of Paul Taylor and Martha Graham.

Today, most ballet companies have a repertoire of works culled or created from a wide variety of dance disciplines. The Royal Danish Ballet preserves its nineteenth-century Bournonville heritage while inviting the modern dance choreographer Murray Louis to create a full-length work about Cleopatra; ballet companies the world over perform José Limón's modern masterpiece *The Moor's Pavane;* the New York-based Joffrey Ballet presents eclectic programs, ranging from the neoclassicism of Balanchine to the rock ballet *Trinity* to Twyla Tharp's latest loose-limbed experiment in fusing ballet with her own idiomatic modern movement.

This peaceful coexistence and cross-pollination on the dance stage has emphasized the dancer's need to be versatile in more than one technique; it has displayed the traditional attributes of the danseur, such as strength and virility, in alliance

with masculine grace and sensitivity. The challenge to ballet by modern dance, though not responsible for the new prominence of the danseur, has effectively increased our flexibility in looking at dance; it has freed us from ballet's strictly formal aesthetics, forcing us to appreciate the artistry involved in the creation of roles. Men who dance may now be called "beautiful," "graceful," and "tender"—adjectives previously reserved strictly for women—without any suggestion of effeminacy or weakness.

Works originally created to display the art of the ballerina during the nineteenth century—which often take their names from the ballerina's role, such as *La Sylphide, Giselle, Coppélia, La Bayadère,* or *Sleeping Beauty*—have undergone an interesting metamorphosis in recent years. These classics, which had fallen out of favor in the early part of our century, are once again the bread and butter of the ballet theater. But audiences are no longer content to see the danseur merely as a handsome foil for the ballerina or to wait until the third act for him to dance. Nureyev and others have added solos, variations, and psychological nuances to their roles in their restaging of such classics as *Raymonda, Swan Lake,* and *The Nutcracker,* so that the essential balance between the male role and that of the ballerina has been restored. If it takes two to tango, by modern standards

15

Above: *Paolo Bortoluzzi as the male protagonist in Maurice Béjart's version of* Firebird, *a work originally created by Michel Fokine for a great ballerina, Tamara Karsavina.* Right: *Erik Bruhn and Violette Verdy in Birgit Cullberg's* Miss Julie. Below: *Ted Nelson as Daedalus and Russell Sultzbach as Icarus, with Ann Marie De Angelo as the Sun, rehearsing the controversial male duet from Gerald Arpino's* The Relativity of Icarus. Opposite: *Marcia Haydée and Richard Cragun, leading dancers of the Stuttgart Ballet, in a breathtaking moment from Glen Tetley's* Voluntaries; *in this dance, the choreographer has combined elements of both ballet and modern dance.*

it also takes two to portray a dramatic love affair—and that, for all their fairy-tale trappings and divertissements, is what most of these ballets are about.

Romantic rapport is also the stuff of which great partnerships are made, and many of history's greatest danseurs have excelled not only as solo artists, but as cavaliers. In no other art form can audiences witness such intense trust—or such fusion of purpose and skill—as in pas de deux performed by supreme artists such as Anton Dolin and Alicia Markova, Rudolf Nureyev and Margot Fonteyn, or Erik Bruhn and Carla Fracci, to name only a few of the great teams of recent decades. These pas de deux become all the more meaningful when the male's role has been strengthened so that his solicitude toward the ballerina makes dramatic sense.

The growing interest in the artistry of the male in ballet and the increasing emphasis on such attributes as virility, grace, and strength have resulted in a conscious search for parallels outside the field of dance, particularly in athletics. The recognition on the playing field of qualities such as grace, beautiful lines of movement, and the flow of arms has been offered as another reason to accept ballet on the same terms that we accept baseball, tennis, or balance beams. At first, these sports parallels appeared to be a public relations gimmick designed to create favorable "masculine" connotations for an art form long associated with women. But the growing popular awareness of the human body as capable of grace and beauty in many of its endeavors, regardless of sex, has made the public conscious of the beauty of all movement, whether performed on a stage, on a playing field, or in a gym class. The acceptance of our bodies and of certain truths about the ways in which we move has helped tremendously in stimulating the popular growth of interest in ballet (and in ballet-related sports, such as ice skating and gymnastics) and in the danseur—ballet's equivalent of the sports hero.

It has become evident that the work of the danseur, who must combine strength, precision, timing, and spatial awareness with grace, musicality, and stage presence, is directly comparable to that of the athlete. Much like athletes, the danseur requires years of training to perfect his form and a daily class routine to warm up his muscles and protect him against an injury that might suddenly end his career. And few sports require the stamina, versatility, and sheer physical daring demanded of the male dancer in ballet today.

For many years there have been a number of different classifications for ranks and physical types among danseurs, although the distinctions are now considered archaic in many companies. Few companies will admit to having a formally structured hierarchy into which dancers and their talents can be

pigeon-holed. This has become especially true since choreography has begun to fit less and less into established categories.

Ballet was born in Italy over 500 years ago, but it grew up in France. There, the language of the classical dance—called *danse d'école*—was codified into a rather arbitrary system, and the steps were given French names that are still in common use. In the language of ballet today, the *premier danseur* is the highest ranking male dancer in a company, as in Britain's Royal Ballet, which has an established structure that includes spots for the principal, soloists, and the members of the corps de ballet. The *danseur étoile* is somewhat removed from this system in that he is that superior performer (the "star" dancer) who may come along once in a generation. The *danseur noble* is a type of dancer with a particularly noble bearing and an elegant line; he is considered not only an excellent dancer in his own right, but the best possible partner for a ballerina.

None of these designations preclude the performance of *demi-caractère* roles, which in addition to classical technique contain dance material derived from sources outside strictly classical ballet—such as national or folk dances; they also require specific types of dramatic characterization, as distinct from the Romantic cavalier. Erik Bruhn, possibly the finest dan-

seur noble of the twentieth century, was capable both of dancing the role of Prince Siegfried in *Swan Lake* and kicking up his heels in a czardas in *Coppélia;* he was also noted for dramatic roles from the contemporary repertoire, such as the butler Jean in *Miss Julie* or Don José in *Carmen*. In recent years, since coming out of a temporary retirement, Bruhn has begun to explore yet another type of role: that of the character dancer, which relies more heavily on dramatic characterization in movement—and even mime—than on classical technique. Among the character roles performed by Bruhn are the witch Madge in *La Sylphide* (a role danced *en travesti*) and the fumbling old Dr. Coppelius in *Coppélia*. (*Demi-caractère* and character dancing, it should be noted, can be performed by women as well as men.)

A thirst for new roles at the top of the ballet hierarchy has quickly filtered down to the men in the corps de ballet, in the form of new demands on their training and skill. When American Ballet Theatre mounts a production of Glen Tetley's *The Rite of Spring* for Mikhail Baryshnikov, it is a test not only of the star's versatility and stamina, but of the abilities of all the men in the company, for the work requires a large contingent of male corps de ballet, as well as other male soloists. It can

Opposite: *Egon Madsen and Reid Anderson of the Stuttgart Ballet rehearsing Kenneth MacMillan's* Requiem *before the watchful eyes of the choreographer (center left).* Far left: *Ballet choreographer Eliot Feld in his own affectionate tribute to the American hoofer,* The Real McCoy. Left: *The great danseur noble Erik Bruhn as Albrecht in Act II of* Giselle. Below: *Richard Cragun and Birgit Keil of the Stuttgart Ballet in* Opus One, *by John Cranko.*

19

he saw the film forty-eight times. Male dancers were then represented on the screen by Fred Astaire and Gene Kelly—the latter with especially strong balletic tendencies, as evidenced in his choreography for *An American in Paris,* as well as in his all-dance film, *Invitation to the Dance.* Nearly thirty years later, three of the world's foremost danseurs are making their mark in films: Nureyev as Rudolf Valentino and Britain's Anthony Dowell as Nijinsky in Ken Russell's *Valentino,* and Baryshnikov as the young danseur in Herbert Ross's *The Turning Point.* The images of the ballerina and of the popular ballroom or jazz dancer are being superseded by that of the great danseur. He in turn, like Shearer, Astaire, and Kelly before him, may influence a whole new generation of aspiring male dancers, who might otherwise have no opportunity to see these stars perform.

Nureyev's name has become a household word, reflecting our interest in dance and especially in the danseur. In the case of Nureyev, and to a rising degree with his "heir apparent," Mikhail Baryshnikov, we have the phenomenon of a unique talent and personality arriving on the entertainment scene at the right moment and fanning the glowing coals of interest into a blazing fire.

The danseur has won the attention of the press, has exerted a magnetic pull at the box office, and has drawn around himself the trappings of a popular cult. Because of the relative ease and convenience of modern transportation, the danseur is able to perform for audiences around the world with regularity, and thereby build a large personal following. Because of the recent liberation of both men and women from sexually stereotyped roles on stage as well as off, the danseur has greater freedom to assert himself in the ballet theater, a theater traditionally dominated by the personality of the ballerina. Because the danseur is, unlike his counterpart in commercial films, a kinetically real, tangible stage presence, the give-and-take relationship established during performance is more immediate and intense for many viewers. And because of the recent infusion of ballet with modern dance, the danseur's technique has been expanded, giving him a greater range and increasing his possibilities for the dramatics and showmanship that so excite the public.

Maurice Béjart, the choreographer of Belgium's Ballet of the Twentieth Century whose views are often controversial, has said that Western civilization experienced a peak in the development of theater in the seventeenth century and of symphonic music in the eighteenth century; the nineteenth century brought opera as a form to its crest; and the twentieth is the century of dance. Yet he might well have claimed more, this man whose company reflects his intense preoccupation with the integral role of the male dancer. For in recent years, all the evidence has pointed to this second half of the twentieth century as becoming the time of the danseur.

even be said that in this and other contemporary works, the danseurs in the corps are given choreography of such difficulty that it would have been considered solo material in years gone by. The highly eclectic, mixed modern and classical repertoires of such companies as the Royal Danish Ballet and The Joffrey Ballet make demands on the male dancer that have never been made before.

Is it merely a coincidence that the tremendous growth in the dance audience corresponds to a large extent with the public's increasing awareness of the male dancer as an artist? In 1950, it was estimated that dance attendance throughout the United States numbered a little over a million and a half people. Only twenty-five years later, this figure had burgeoned to an estimated 11 to 15 million! At the same time, Mikhail Baryshnikov appeared on the covers of America's two leading weekly news publications, both in the same week, only a year after his defection from the Leningrad Kirov Ballet. This reflects a public appetite that has grown to proportions of feast—if not gluttony.

Look at the coverage given to dance in other media, and you will understand the scope of today's avid interest in the art. Children's programs on television deal with the prowess and nobility of ballet in the same terms used to describe a sports event, while full-length ballet classics are being aired on television during prime time.

Ballet has made perhaps an even greater impact through the movies. *The Red Shoes* is a British film that appeared in 1948 with the ballerina Moira Shearer in the starring role; focusing on the backstage life and career of a young dancer, it influenced innumerable young people to study dance—among them, the Dutch choreographer Rudi van Dantzig, who claims

Above: Edward Villella, a prominent American danseur. Opposite: *Dutch choreographer Hans van Manen rehearsing Anthony Dowell, premier danseur of Britain's Royal Ballet, in van Manen's lyrical* Four Schumann Pieces.

2

Sun King
to Swan Song

The contemporary popularity of male dancers such as Nureyev and Baryshnikov is by no means unique in the history of ballet, although the current interest is spread over a broader segment of the population than during the time of Louis XIV. Ballet takes its name from *ballo,* a dance of fifteenth-century Italy, one of the earliest dances to be formally composed and set to a specific piece of music. Ballet reached its first flowering during the long opulent reign of the French monarch Louis XIV (1643–1715).

From the time that he was a young man, Louis was devoted to his court ballets, seeing in them a means of entertaining his restless courtiers, promoting political ideologies, and impressing foreign dignitaries. As a dancer—when he was young—and as a royal patron and entrepreneur, long after he had grown too stout to dance himself, Louis's abiding affection for dance would make it possible to codify the steps; by 1672, he had established a school for music and dance in which ballet would flourish for centuries, into our own times. Louis's epithet, *Le Roi Soleil*—the Sun King—comes from a role he danced at age fifteen in *Le Ballet Royal de la Nuit,* a court ballet in four parts and forty-three scenes that lasted a staggering thirteen hours. Louis appeared as the Sun, replete with a sun symbol on his chest and rays around his head, neck, shoulders, wrists, knees, and shoes. As the bringer of light, Louis's role had significant political implications, for the young monarch was being portrayed as the shining savior of France, which had been suffering from the darkness of civil war.

During these formative years of ballet, the dancing stage was dominated by men. Male courtiers during Louis's time assumed the women's roles, dancing *en travesti* (literally, in disguise), since it was not acceptable for a well-bred woman to appear on stage in public. Also, the male dancer's costume allowed him a greater freedom of movement and therefore greater virtuosity than a woman could hope to achieve, hampered as she was by a long, full skirt. And so, while a certain Mlle. Lafontaine became the first professional woman dancer of

record in 1681, she presented no challenge to the ascendant male. The stars of the day were men such as Pierre Beauchamp, Jean Balon, and Louis Dupré. Beauchamp was not only a brilliant dancer but a choreographer as well. Balon is said to have been the greatest dancer in Europe, renowned for his extraordinary lightness of movement; it is often assumed that his name gives us the term *ballon,* which refers to a dancer's ability to appear to remain in the air a long time. Dupré, known as "Le Grand Dupré" or even "the God of the Dance," was considered the model of the danseur noble.

By the time of Louis XIV, court ballet had evolved into a chain of dances loosely linked around a theme, usually mythological. It was performed by courtiers and was characterized by stately movements that formed geometric patterns on the floor. The professional dancer had not yet emerged, but would soon do so with the growth of dancing academies throughout Europe. Until then, performances were given by the king and his courtiers, with the dancing masters performing the virtuosic material. The style of these performances must have been stately and elegant, sometimes spirited, having evolved from court dances that dated back to the early years of the Renaissance—the pavane, the galliard, the volta, the gigue, the sarabande, and the bourrée—which themselves had developed from folk dances.

Louis's dancing master, Pierre Beauchamp, began recording this highly stylized court dancing during the 1660s, formulating what would become our *danse d'école,* the classical technique whose principles are still focal points in the scheme of ballet today. These principles included the "turned-out" leg, with the dancer's body facing the audience in such a manner that maximum silhouetting was achieved, and the five positions of the feet. Beauchamp's elevation (ability to leap into the air) and turns were the basis of today's virtuoso techniques, such as pirouettes and *tours en l'air;* and they soon marked a turning point in the development of ballet. Courtiers devoting only

Apollon ——— le Roy

Preceding pages: *Mikhail Baryshnikov and Merle Park in the nineteenth-century classic* Swan Lake. Left: *Louis XIV, the Sun King, as Apollo.* Below: *A drawing of Gaetan Vestris in Jean-Georges Noverre's* Jason and Medea. Bottom: *Baryshnikov in two moments from* Vestris, *a modern evocation of the eighteenth-century virtuoso Auguste Vestris.*

25

Above: *Baryshnikov in a spectacular leap from* Vestris. Opposite:
*Michael Coleman, a leading danseur with Britain's Royal Ballet, as
Colas in Sir Frederick Ashton's version of* La Fille Mal Gardée.

leisure time to the dance could not compete with the growing number of full-time, professional dancers (nor did they wish to do so, given the traditional aristocratic distaste for professionalism). Ballet had become not only an art for the entertainment of princes, but a career.

It was inevitable that in the first half of the eighteenth century a woman, Marie Camargo, would think of shortening her skirt and removing the heels from her shoes to show that she, too, had feet that could perform a twinkling *entrechat quatre,* a difficult step that involved rising vertically and crossing her feet back and forth in the air two times before coming down again. Another woman, an Italian dancer known as Barberina, soon surpassed this by performing an *entrechat huit,* the same step performed with eight movements. These were the female technicians of the time. Another dancer of the period,

Marie Sallé, gained notoriety in the 1730s for her scandalously simplified costumes and her delicate, dramatic approach to dance. But although Camargo, Barberina, and Sallé successfully entered the male preserve of ballet and their names are remembered, their careers offered only a small challenge to male supremacy in dance.

During the eighteenth century, two dancers, Gaetan Vestris and his son Auguste, led the field of danseurs: when they appeared together in London in 1781, Parliament interrupted its session so that its members might see them dance. The elder Vestris was a great mime actor whose most famous vehicle was *Jason and Medea,* in which he danced the role of Jason. The only dancer he acknowledged to be greater than himself was his son, a virtuoso noted for turns and jumps; something of his style can be seen in the solo *Vestris,* created for Mikhail Barysh-

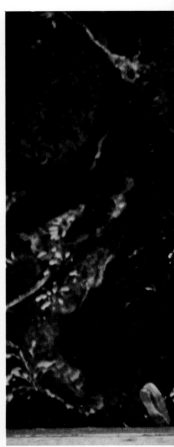

Opposite: *Stanley Holden of the Royal Ballet as the Widow Simone in the clog dance from Ashton's* La Fille Mal Gardée. Above: *In The Joffrey's production of* The Dream, *inspired by Shakespeare's* A Midsummer Night's Dream, *Larry Grenier as Bottom demonstrates to comic effect that men, too, can dance on pointe.* Left: *Erik Bruhn as the idealist James and Carla Fracci as the ethereal Sylphide of his dreams in Bournonville's* La Sylphide, *a ballet that was closely associated with these two dancers during the years of their partnership.*

Various stagings of Bournonville's Romantic classic La Sylphide. *Above:* Neils Bjorn Larsen of the Royal Danish Ballet as Madge the Witch, who engineers James's tragic fate. *Opposite:* Gelsey Kirkland in the title role and Mikhail Baryshnikov as James entranced by the playful Sylphide, in Act II of Erik Bruhn's production for American Ballet Theatre. Baryshnikov had never danced Bournonville's choreography before coming to the West, but he was eager to perform the role of James. He was coached in the Bournonville style—very different from his own Russian classical technique—by Bruhn, a great exponent of the Danish Bournonville tradition.

nikov by Leonid Jacobson in 1969. This seven-minute cameo ballet consists of seven dance-mime episodes, representing "An Old Man Dancing the Minuet," "The Coquette Dance," "The Preacher-Prophet," "Classical Dance Variations," "Prayer," "Laughter," and "Dying Man." The titles speak for themselves. The youthful Baryshnikov, in white wig and satin costume, performs these episodes to an eighteenth-century musical pastiche in the spirit of the young Vestris, whose art was visually recorded in numerous old drawings.

Although little of the actual choreography and technique has survived from the first 150 years of ballet, contemporary choreographers and dance historians have made imaginative reconstructions of what they must have been like. These reconstructions are based on the music, art, and costume of the period, as well as on purely social dances such as the courante and the minuet. Although the steps of both the formally composed court ballets and the purely social dances (on which they were based) were notated, the art of dancing has been preserved mostly as a physical tradition, being passed on by direct demonstration from generation to generation. Even today, roles and new technical achievements are usually preserved only when they are taught by teacher to student or by one dancer to another.

From the late seventeenth to the early nineteenth century, the virtuosity and popularity of the male dancer reached a peak not attained again until the middle of the twentieth century. At the same time, there was a rise in the number of ballet schools and companies and a desire to pass along technique from teacher to pupil and to record the methods being taught. In this way, it is possible to trace certain styles of dancing from the present back two centuries, or even farther. A remarkable chain of knowledge exists, linking "Le Grand Dupré" to Auguste Vestris to dancers of our own time. To have studied with Vestris or Dupré was to have worked with the most famous ballet teachers of the eighteenth century. A similar reverence for teachers exists today, so that when one hears of a dancer having trained at a particular academy with a particular teacher, more often than not one will know about the kind of dancer he is.

By the mid-eighteenth century, with the increased emphasis on achieving more sparkling and dramatic technical feats, a great number of innovative and demanding movements were added to ballet's vocabulary of steps. These movements required even more intensive training, better schools, and a new format in which to display the dancers' accomplishments. The old ballet was principally a series of divertissements strung loosely together around a theme, which was usually mythological or pastoral. With the development of rationalist and humanist philosophy in the course of the Enlightenment, these themes came to seem artificial and meaningless. People began to re-

Scenes from Giselle. Below: *Anthony Dowell and Antoinette Sibley as happy lovers before Albrecht's duplicity is discovered.* Right: *Albrecht (Mikhail Baryshnikov) pleads with the heartbroken Giselle (Gelsey Kirkland).* Bottom left: *Giselle's mad scene, with Carla Fracci and Erik Bruhn.* Bottom right: *Rudolf Nureyev as Albrecht brings lilies to Giselle's grave in the forest.*

32

quire more rational frameworks for their ballets, and dance began to shift from the merely decorative to the narrative and the dramatic.

Among the most successful early efforts with the new *ballet d'action,* as these increasingly dramatic dance works were known, was *The Loves of Mars and Venus,* by the brilliant English dancing master John Weaver. It premiered in London in 1717 with an all-English cast, except for the presence of the French dancer Louis Dupré, known today both as the prototype of the danseur noble and as the teacher of Jean-Georges Noverre. Weaver eliminated speaking roles entirely from the ballet stage, replacing words with gesture and mime.

Noverre was an even more important dancer and choreographer who is considered to be the principal exponent of the *ballet d'action.* Called "the Shakespeare of the dance" by the famous English actor David Garrick, Noverre set down principles in his fifteen *Lettres sur la Danse et sur les Ballets* (1760) that remain the cornerstones of theater dance in our own time. He and his pupils were largely responsible for the elimination of masks from the ballet stage and for replacing the conventionalized movements and gestures of ballet with more natural styles of performing; believable plot-lines and gestures revealing genuine emotions were emphasized. Noverre's most famous pupil was Jean Dauberval, who gave us one of the most typical of the new ballets, *La Fille Mal Gardée,* which received its premiere performance in 1789, the year of the Revolution.

Fille, as it is fondly known, is one of the earliest works to survive on our contemporary ballet stage (though it has lost its original choreography by Dauberval). It is a clear statement favoring the common man, and it stands in sharp contrast to the classical ideals that had characterized many popular ballets of the period. *Fille* has no mythological demons or wispy naiads, no gods descending from clouds, no declamation praising the king or an honored guest. Rather, it is a story of country life and romance, having as its protagonists a pair of young lovers who outwit the older generation, which believes in marriages of convenience, not of love.

As a forerunner of the Romantic movement that soon engulfed all of European culture, and especially ballet, *Fille* was performed on the stages of Europe—with a special popularity in England—until the mid-nineteenth century; in 1848, it gained a new lease on life in St. Petersburg when Fanny Elssler danced there in a new production. Russia was in fact to be the main scene of the ballet's survival. Some of the greatest ballerinas in history, including Anna Pavlova, have performed the title role of Lise and been partnered by a series of great danseurs portraying Colas, the romantic young hero of the ballet. But much of the fun that audiences continue to experience in watching *La Fille Mal Gardée* is generated by the two character roles given to male dancers: the Widow Simone, traditionally performed *en travesti,* and Lise's endearingly idiotic suitor, Alain, who at one point vainly bounds about the stage with a butterfly net. In 1960, Sir Frederick Ashton mounted a new version of *Fille* with Britain's Royal Ballet, a production highlighted by Stanley Holden as the Widow, in a clog dance that stopped the show, and by Alexander Grant's brilliant performance as Alain.

Toward the end of the eighteenth and well into the middle of the nineteenth centuries, the spirit of revolution arose throughout Europe—revolution against monarchies, religion, classicism (the neo-Greek and neo-Roman taste that arose during the 1700s), as well as against the rapid increase of industrialization and the rise of science. Romanticism became a part of this web of rebellion, expressing the ideals that men sought, as well as the harsh and often tragic realities that made the ideals often unattainable. The effect on ballet was to idealize the female roles, while the men became dreamers, ready to sacrifice their lives for the Romantic ideal. By the mid-1830s, sylphs and other ethereal, supernatural creatures of the Romantic imagination filled the stages of Europe. There, the new gas lighting made it possible to achieve a wide range of moods on stage, from sparkling, sunny scenes to dismal gloom in haunted abbeys or threatening forests. The great deluge of new middle-class patrons at the ballet gave rise to balletomanes, whose theatrical taste favored the grotesque, the mysterious, the fantastic—anything, in fact, that helped to turn their thoughts from the real world. The ballerina, clad in diaphanous muslin and the new flesh-colored tights, symbolized the ethereal ideal, so chaste and otherworldly that she seemed to float through the air.

Early in the nineteenth century, danseurs still captured the lion's share of public attention, because of both their greater virtuosity and the social structure of the day, in which great doings and large events were the prerogatives of men. During the pre-Romantic period, leading male dancers included Charles-Louis Didelot (who suspended his dancers by wires to achieve the illusion of flight), Salvatore Viganō (whose career as dancer and choreographer coincided with the greatest period of ballet in Italy), and Carlo Blasis. Blasis, an Italian choreographer and premier danseur, wrote two important textbooks, which were published during the 1820s and remain, to this day, the basic works on the fundamentals of classical dance.

Male technique, however, was soon to be eclipsed by the combination of Romanticism, which favored female characters, and a dramatic occurrence in ballet history: the development of pointe work, in which women danced on the tips of their toes.

Toe dancing as we know it today was not possible for any sustained performing until the invention late in the nineteenth

century of the toe shoe (which is darned and glued for added support of the ballerina's foot), but Marie Taglioni was able to perform an approximation of toe dancing, and the audiences went wild. The male did not counter with an equally stunning stage effect, although a school of teaching today claims that there is no anatomical reason why men can't dance on pointe —in fact, in some ballets they do. In 1924, Anton Dolin startled French audiences by dancing on pointe in Nijinska's *Les Facheux;* and in Sir Frederick Ashton's *The Dream,* an adaptation of Shakespeare, the danseur portraying Bottom dances on pointe to create the illusion of hooves during his temporary transformation into an ass.

In any case, pointe work for a time extended the technical range of both male and female dancers while its implications for partnering were being explored. But with the premiere of *La Sylphide* in Paris in 1832, the supremacy of the male in ballet was eclipsed. Marie Taglioni in the title role both established the

mystique of the ballerina and made toe dancing the rage of Europe. Théophile Gautier, preeminent dance critic of the Romantic age, wrote that "Dance has as its sole object the revelation of beautiful form, in graceful attitudes and the development of lines that are pleasing to the eye. . . . Nothing is more abominable than a man who displays a red neck, great muscular arms, legs with calves like a church beadle, his whole heavy frame shaken with leaps and pirouettes. . . . [Men] affect that false grace, those revolting manners that have sickened the public of male dancing."

It should be noted that Gautier's assessment comes after the decline of good male dancers had begun; it is possible that prejudice had already driven away men with talent and that Gautier was describing accurately what was left—a passel of poor dancers. A far cry from Voltaire's praise of Marie Camargo nearly a century earlier, when he said that she was the first woman to dance like a man!

Opposite: *Burton Taylor as Arthur Saint-Léon, surrounded by Francesca Corkle as Cerrito, Denise Jackson as Taglioni, and Charthel Arthur as Grahn, in Robert Joffrey's* Pas des Déesses, *inspired by nineteenth-century lithographs of the Romantic ballet. Below: An early print of Lucile Grahn and Jules Perrot, one of the few danseurs to achieve prominence during the Romantic period. Moments from Act II of* Giselle. *Left: In rehearsal, Natalia Makarova in the title role comforts Erik Bruhn as Albrecht, shielding him from the wilis. Bottom: The Bolshoi's Mikhail Lavrovsky as Albrecht visits the grave of Giselle, while she (Natalia Bessmertnova) appears to him as a wili.*

Scenes from Coppélia. *Top: Erik Bruhn as Frantz kicks up his heels in a czardas, in the village celebration from Act I. Above: More recently, Bruhn has performed the character role of the mysterious Dr. Coppelius, who experiments with bringing dolls to life. He is seen here with Rudolf Nureyev as the sleeping Frantz (right) and Veronica Tennant, of the National Ballet of Canada, as Swanilda, pretending to be one of Coppelius's dolls. Opposite: Mikhail Baryshnikov as Frantz dances at his wedding to Swanilda, in the ballet's happy conclusion.*

The original *La Sylphide* (which is not the version seen today) was choreographed by Filippo Taglioni, the father of Marie and also her teacher, determined to make her the greatest ballerina in the world. Everything he could do to minimize her physical flaws (she had long, thin arms) and emphasize her best qualities (he devised brilliant combinations of leaps and bounds to develop the ethereal lightness that was her greatest asset) became permanently enshrined in the traditions of Romantic ballet.

Overnight, Marie Taglioni became a legend. The ballet that will be forever associated with her name, *La Sylphide,* set the taste for what came to be called ballet blanc, which featured a corps de ballet of graceful ballerinas dancing in flowing white skirts. Taglioni's *Sylphide* costume, attributed to Eugene Lami, came to be the standard for Romantic ballet: a tight-fitting bodice, with bare shoulders and neck, and a white muslin skirt in layers reaching below the knee.

In retrospect, it seems logical that the finest danseur of the period, Jules Perrot, a frequent partner of Taglioni, should have been cast opposite her in *La Sylphide* in the role of James; but the role was in fact first performed by a comparatively unknown danseur named Joseph Mazilier. Why? It seems that, for Taglioni's debut in the trend-setting ballet, Perrot was too good; Marie was jealous of his fame. Backstage politics, which by this time had become rife with favoritism, resulted in Mazilier's selection. Not only in the estimation of the public, but in the eyes of the management as well, the male dancer was consciously diminished.

La Sylphide expresses a basic theme of the Romantics. The first act is a festive occasion, set in Scotland, in which James's forthcoming marriage to the village girl Effie is being celebrated; the second act takes place in a moonlit forest to which the Sylphide draws James for the ballet's tragic conclusion. James is the dreamer who falls in love with an ideal—the idealized woman embodied in the Sylphide—and the tragedy lies in his abandoning reality in pursuit of the unattainable. When he finally embraces the elusive Sylphide during the forest scene, he uses a scarf that, unknown to him, has been poisoned by a witch. The Sylphide's wings drop off, she dies, and is borne away through the treetops by her sister-sylphides. James is left alone with his grief.

La Sylphide was an enormous personal triumph for Marie Taglioni, and its influence was felt throughout the course of Romantic ballet, establishing the ballerina as goddess of the dance. But it survives on ballet stages today as more than a historical landmark or a "period" curiosity. The great dancer and choreographer August Bournonville saw the work in Paris, and when he returned home to Copenhagen in 1836, he staged

his own version of it, one that is still performed in Denmark—and by companies the world over—to this day.

The success of Bournonville's version is due not only to his choreographic genius but also to his balancing of the interest in the roles of the Sylphide and James. Himself a brilliant technician, excelling in batterie and steps of elevation, Bournonville championed the equality between the roles of the danseur and the ballerina (as well as the acceptance of the dancer as a respectable citizen) throughout the forty-odd years he spent as choreographer for the Royal Danish Ballet. Both his ballets and his teaching methods provided the only safe haven for male dancing throughout the nineteenth century. They produced the great nineteenth-century danseur Christian Johansson, who went on to become a brilliant and important teacher in his own right in Russia, thus influencing the performance style we see now in Russian ballet; they have also produced some of the major male dancers of our own time, including Erik Bruhn, Henning Kronstam, Niels Kehlet, Egon Madsen, and Peter Martins. Bournonville's methods and his ballets are lovingly preserved in Denmark today. Now that the male dancer has come into his own again, excerpts and even whole acts from such full-length Bournonville ballets as *Konservatoriet, La Ventana,* and *Napoli* are eagerly being acquired by companies the world over as challenges to their dancers' technique.

Giselle, or the Wilis, which premiered in Paris in 1841, was an even greater Romantic triumph than *La Sylphide,* and today it is considered one of the two ballets most challenging to the ballerina's art (the other being *Swan Lake*). That it is the quintessential ballet of the era is unquestionable, for it contains those elements of conflict so essential to the Romantics: light against dark, good against evil, life against death, daylight against moonlight. The work has survived with an unbroken record of performance to the present day at least partly because it provides a role of almost equal importance for the danseur—that of the nobleman Albrecht, who loves but deceives the heroine, Giselle. The greatest ballerinas in dance history have essayed the title role, but the list of danseurs who have been their partners is equally impressive: Lucien Petipa, premier danseur of the Paris Opera, at the ballet's premiere with Carlotta Grisi; Nijinsky with Tamara Karsavina; Anton Dolin with Alicia Markova; Igor Youskevitch with Alicia Alonso; and Erik Bruhn, Rudolf Nureyev, and Mikhail Baryshnikov with numerous partners in recent years.

Giselle was conceived by Théophile Gautier—the same writer who found men an abomination on the ballet stage—as a vehicle for Carlotta Grisi, with whom he had fallen in love; and it was for Grisi that her husband—the great danseur of the age, Jules Perrot—created Giselle's dances. Gautier's story was suggested by a poem by Heinrich Heine, which in turn was based on folk legend dealing with the fearsome wilis (related, in Slavic countries, to vampires). Wilis are the spirits of maidens who have died untimely deaths because they were betrayed by their lovers. As lovely ghosts, they take vengeance on the male sex by dancing to death any man unwise enough to cross their path between midnight and sunrise. What sets *Giselle* apart from previous ballets is the establishment of the heroine as a real person: a happy peasant girl who goes mad when she learns of Albrecht's duplicity and dies tragically. When she reappears as a shade in the second act, forgiving Albrecht and rescuing him from the wilis, the audience is satisfied that she has a basis in real life, unlike the Sylphide, who may be only a figment of the hero's imagination from the start.

If over the years there have been variations in the interpretation of Giselle's character, there has been an equally wide exploration of Albrecht's motive in betraying her. In most productions of the ballet, the danseur has little to do but partner Giselle in the first act, but he must nevertheless be convincing in the portrayal of some rather complex emotions. His opportunity to dance, compelled by the wilis who have caught him mourning by Giselle's grave in the forest, comes in the second.

Erik Bruhn, who was closely identified with the role throughout his career, interpreted Albrecht as a playboy who never dreams that Giselle will take him so seriously, but who matures after her death through the recognition and acceptance of his guilt. Nureyev's Albrecht was highly controversial when he first performed the role at Covent Garden in 1962. In place of the dashing romantic hero then fashionable in the West, he gave us the naturalistic Russian interpretation of the character: a passionate, selfish young aristocrat who experiences real remorse at Giselle's tragic fate. But although Nureyev's performance made dramatic sense of the role and was therefore acceptable, his interpolation of different choreography for Albrecht in the second act—particularly his introduction of a solo for Albrecht in the midst of the wilis (now widely copied)—was much criticized, even as his technique in the traditional cabrioles and other solo passages was being highly praised. The more recent Russian defector, Mikhail Baryshnikov, who chose the role of Albrecht for his American debut in 1974, reacts with a frenzy of guilt and grief at Giselle's death that rivals the intense drama of her mad scene moments before; at the end of the ballet, he is saved from the wilis only to be left in despair at the second—and final—loss of Giselle.

By the time of *Giselle,* which perfected the Romantic formula, the ranks of distinguished male dancers had been reduced to a handful. The overwhelming attention of balletomanes was now squarely on the new ballerinas—those airborne

Moments from Swan Lake. Left: *Natalia Makarova and Ivan Nagy of American Ballet Theatre, often paired in the classics, are seen here as the Swan Queen Odette and Prince Siegfried in the last act. Siegfried has been tricked by Odile into betraying his vow of fidelity to Odette, and the lovers despair of breaking the sorceror Von Rothbart's spell.* Below left: *Birgit Keil (Odile) and Richard Cragun (Siegfried) of Germany's Stuttgart Ballet in the Black Swan Pas de Deux.* Below: *Erik Bruhn as Prince Siegfried and Celia Franca as the Black Queen in Bruhn's production for the National Ballet of Canada.*

creatures who danced on their toes, seeming to sum up all the idealized charms of the fair sex—leaving ballet in an unfortunate state of sexual imbalance. Some of the most lyrical movement in ballet is adagio dancing—slow, sustained phrases in which the ballerina is partnered by the danseur. In classical ballet, *adagio* usually refers to the pas de deux, the duet danced by the male and female leads, in which the emphasis is on beauty and purity of line and in which the usual emotion expressed is love. When the idolization of nineteenth-century ballerinas pushed the male dancer out of the spotlight, the male-female relationship that provided a real-life framework for the audience to identify with was destroyed.

The names of very few great danseurs come down to us from this period. Jules Perrot, the choreographer of Grisi's dances in *Giselle,* was a danseur who overcame the handicaps of a singularly ugly face and an ill-proportioned upper body. He was not only one of the most important choreographers of the mid-nineteenth century, but also one of the few male dancers of the age who was popular with both the public and the critics. He began his career in Lyons as a child acrobat and grotesque mime. As the result of a visit in 1823 to Paris, when he was in his early teens, he conceived the ambition to become a great classical dancer, and to that end he studied with Auguste Vestris. He heeded his teacher's advice to "Turn, spin, fly, but never give the public time to examine your person closely." As the frequent partner of Marie Taglioni, his style was greatly influenced by her quickness, lightness, and grace—skills that were congenial to his own abilities. Théophile Gautier, in *The Romantic Ballet,* describes Perrot in *Le Zingaro* (1840; a ballet-opera Perrot had helped to write) as "the male Taglioni! . . . Perrot displays perfect grace, purity, and lightness: it is music made visible . . . his legs sing very agreeably to the eye. These praises are the less to be doubted coming from us, since there is nothing we like less than to see male dancers."

Perrot's career suffered a severe setback when Taglioni's backstage machinations kept him from performing as her partner in the premiere of *La Sylphide.* Although there were great roles and triumphs before him across Europe, his virtual exclusion from what was then the highest citadel of dance—the Paris Opera—was a disappointment that would rankle him for much of his life. He was unsuccessful in his attempt to regain a foothold at the Opera in 1841, when he brought his wife, the ballerina Carlotta Grisi, to Paris. She made a successful debut at the Opera and scored a triumph shortly thereafter in *Giselle,* but Perrot, far from being invited back to perform, was not even credited for the beautiful and innovative choreography he did for her dances. In later years, Perrot was associated with all the great ballerinas of the age, as well as with one of the period's greatest theater coups: the creation in London of the brilliant

Pas de Quatre, a diplomatic and choreographic tour de force composed for the rival ballerinas Taglioni, Grisi, Fanny Cerrito, and Lucile Grahn, each of whom needed to be satisfied that her role was as exciting and brilliant as that of the other three, if not more so. The final and possibly most influential phase of his career was spent in Russia, which he visited for the first time in 1848. He worked there quite steadily, restaging his already successful ballets and occasionally creating new ones, until 1859, when he retired and returned to France, to live there in relative obscurity until his death in 1892. A choreographer in the tradition of Noverre and Noverre's pupils Charles-Louis Didelot and Jean Dauberval, with a brilliant technique and a flair for creating dramatic situations on stage, Perrot was one of the most important figures in nineteenth-century ballet.

As a dancer, Arthur Saint-Léon is perhaps best remembered as the partner of one of the greatest Romantic ballerinas, Fanny Cerrito; it was he who partnered Cerrito, Taglioni, and Grahn in the 1846 *Pas des Déesses* by Perrot, on which Robert Joffrey has based his own *Pas des Déesses.* But it is primarily as a choreographer that Saint-Léon is known today. While serving as ballet master in St. Petersburg, the successor to Perrot, Saint-Léon created *The Little Humpbacked Horse,* the first ballet with a Russian theme and one that is still popular, although with new choreography, in Russia today. His final ballet, produced at the Paris Opera in 1870, was his masterwork: *Coppélia, or the Girl with the Enamel Eyes,* one of the staples of the international ballet repertoire.

Coppélia is an important work in tracing the fortunes of the male in ballet because in its original form it serves as a symbol of the nadir of the danseur's popularity. By 1870, men had all but vanished from the ballet stage in Western Europe; the vogue was for women who looked well in tights to replace them in their roles. In a tradition that has survived well into the twentieth century at the Paris Opera, the role of Frantz, the young man who loves the heroine, Swanilda, was performed *en travestie* by Eugénie Fiocre. When Swanilda required partnering in a pas de deux, a gentleman of the corps stepped forward and supported her.

In recent decades, however, Frantz has become an important role for the danseur, and has been danced with much success by Frederic Franklin, in partnership with a famous Swanilda, Alexandra Danilova; Erik Bruhn; Rudolf Nureyev, who essayed the role as one of his first comic creations; Mikhail Baryshnikov; and Fernando Bujones, among others. Perhaps the most distinguished new production of the ballet in some years is that staged by Danilova and George Balanchine for the New York City Ballet in 1975, with Helgi Tomasson partnering Patricia McBride. Since coming out of a premature retirement in 1975, Bruhn has given some memorable performances in the

Natalia Makarova as the Princess Aurora and Rudolf Nureyev as Prince Florimund in the pas de deux from the last act of Sleeping Beauty.

In the simple story of the original
Nutcracker, *created by Petipa and
Ivanov in St. Petersburg in 1892,
Clara—performed by a little girl—
dreams that her Christmas nutcracker
is transformed into a cavalier.
Rudolf Nureyev's 1967 production of*
The Nutcracker *for the Royal Ballet
dispensed with Clara as a child; the
role was performed by a ballerina, who
dances the grand pas de deux with
godfather Drosselemeyer, who becomes a
cavalier in Clara's dream of the
Kingdom of Sweets.* Above: *Nureyev as
Drosselemeyer relaxes backstage with
Merle Park as Clara and other members
of the cast from that production.*
Right: *Mikhail Baryshnikov and
Marianna Tcherkassky in Baryshnikov's
production of* The Nutcracker *for
American Ballet Theatre.* Opposite:
*Vyacheslav Gordeyev and Ludmila
Semenyaka of the Bolshoi Ballet in
the Bluebird Pas de Deux from
Sleeping Beauty.*

other important male role in the ballet, that of Dr. Coppelius, the mysterious old dollmaker. In the hands of a consummate actor, this role becomes a brilliant tour de force of mime, and Bruhn follows in the tradition of Enrico Cecchetti and Robert Helpmann, that master of stage makeup, both of whom will long be associated with the part.

The choreography of *Coppélia* has been greatly revised over the years, the version we know today being for the most part the Russian one with choreography by Lev Ivanov and Enrico Cecchetti, itself based on Marius Petipa's 1884 choreography for the ballet. It is a sparkling, light-hearted work, with much humor and rejoicing to replace the ethereal spirits, gloom, and unrequited love of previous ballets. Its story, music, and spirit are a delightfully upbeat conclusion to the end of the Romantic era in ballet. And with its introduction of the Hungarian czardas and other folk dances, *Coppélia* points the way to the adaptation for ballet of national dances in other ballets —such as the Russian classics *Swan Lake* and *The Nutcracker* —which gave ballet a new variety of steps and new opportunities for male dancers to shine. Moreover, the sunny symphonic score by Delibes, with its national flavors, danceable melodies, and orchestral "descriptions" of the principal characters, was an enormous breakthrough in composition for the ballet stage, soon to be favored by one of the greatest ballet composers of all time, Peter Ilyitch Tchaikovsky.

It is difficult to extend Romanticism beyond *Coppélia,* the last ballet produced at the Paris Opera before that institution was closed by the Franco-Prussian War. By the 1870s ballet in France had declined to something little better than a high-class girlie show, in which brigades of girl sailors and soldiers pranced across the stage in leg-enhancing tights. A new era—that of the "classical" ballet—had already gained a foothold elsewhere. Nurtured by Perrot and his successor, Saint-Léon, ballet had found a home in czarist Russia, where the softness and lyricism of the Romantics yielded to the brilliant and technically exacting spectacles choreographed in St. Petersburg by Marius Petipa, who was to be the dominant force in ballet until his retirement in 1903.

During the years of Petipa's influence, which spanned almost half a century, Russian classical ballet reached a dazzling

zenith with the production of such full-length works as *La Baya-dère, Raymonda, Swan Lake, Sleeping Beauty,* and that perennial Christmas favorite, *The Nutcracker.* This period also had a tremendous influence on ballet development and training in the twentieth century, especially in England and America, where to this day ballet schooling can be traced back to Imperial Russia before the turn of the century.

Why Russia? There are numerous reasons, many of them political. When, in 1700, Peter the Great determined that Russia should enter the "modern age," he quite naturally created a welcome atmosphere for ballet and court dancing, which was all the rage in France at that time. When ballet finally became established on Russian soil, it had the almost unqualified support of the czar, who paid all the bills and made the ballet company in St. Petersburg a part of the imperial household. As educated people, and as functionaries operating in a civil service capacity directly under the czar's supervision, the dancers were held in a certain esteem; to become a dancer was not only an honor, it was also one of the few ways in which a common person might raise his social standing and be assured of a regular income.

The total subsidy for dance, which continued even after the 1917 Revolution, enabled the Russian system of teaching to become a model of efficiency and artistic achievement; today it provides the best ballet training available (although dance in the Soviet Union remains isolated from some of the greatest developments in modern ballet). In the careers of male dancers such as the Bolshoi's Vladimir Vasiliev and Maris Liepa, or the Leningrad Kirov Ballet's former danseurs Rudolf Nureyev and Mikhail Baryshnikov, we can see the strong male qualities fostered in dance, in a country where men in ballet are accepted as artists and are often honored by the state. If such acceptance and honor have not been enough for Nureyev and Baryshnikov, it is not a reflection of their political ideals, they claim, but of their desire to perform more than the great nineteenth-century classics and the propagandistic spectacles of contemporary Russian ballet.

A fresh and authentically Russian perspective on the late-nineteenth-century classics has been given us by a number of Russian émigrés, just as the treasure trove of male dancing in the Danish Bournonville repertoire has been opened up to us by the international career of Erik Bruhn and the travels of the Royal Danish Ballet. The Russian ballet master Serge Grigoriev staged the famous production of *Sleeping Beauty* presented by Diaghilev's Ballets Russes in London in 1921. Nureyev, Natalia Makarova, and Baryshnikov have produced lesser-known classics such as *Don Quixote, Raymonda,* and *La Bayadère* (the fourth act, known as the "Kingdom of the Shades"), making these ballets almost as much staple items of the Western reper-

toire as are *The Nutcracker* and *Swan Lake.* These ballets are still rightly considered vehicles for our great ballerinas, just as they were for earlier dancers. But in the choreographically augmented versions seen today, they also provide ample performing opportunities for the danseur.

Marius Petipa, the French choreographer-in-chief at the St. Petersburg Imperial Theatre from 1862 until 1903, was the mastermind behind the original productions of these classics and might well be called the Cecil B. DeMille of the ballet. His dance spectacles routinely incorporated elements of the deeply rooted Russian traditions of folk dance, character dances, and passages of mime to offset the ballet blanc, or pure dance, sequences. From Perrot, his chief mentor, Petipa had absorbed a skill in handling dramatic incident. His themes were often derived from news items of fashionable interest, and they were always treated with his particular audience in mind, whether it was the aristocrats of St. Petersburg or the middle class of Moscow, who preferred a good dramatic story told in dance to the pure classicism favored by the Court. His formula for producing a ballet—from top to bottom, as it were, since he involved himself in every aspect of production, from sets, to costumes, to score—scarcely varied throughout his career. It was his equal genius in setting dances on the corps de ballet and in creating pas de deux that makes us refer to Petipa as the father of the classical ballet. His works are an enduring, major part of the repertoire today.

From a modern standpoint, however, Petipa had two rather serious flaws. The stories of a great many of his works are hopelessly, even dottily convoluted by our standards, and these ballets for the most part have not survived—or else their plots have been heavily reworked and often overlaid with a bit of Freudian psychology, as is the case with Nureyev's production of *Raymonda* for American Ballet Theatre. Petipa's other weakness was his lack of interest in creating dances for men.

Petipa may never have proclaimed to the world at large that "Ballet is woman"—the words of the great twentieth-century choreographer George Balanchine, product of St. Petersburg's Imperial School of Ballet. But the truth is that he much preferred working with ballerinas, making them the focal points of his ballets. Yet although the male dancer under Petipa's regime did not share the ballerina's popularity either with the maestro or with the public, he often had the opportunity to show his virtuosity in the character and mime roles that were included in the sprawling ballet-spectacles. Perhaps recognizing his own shortcomings, Petipa often turned the male dancers over to Christian Johansson (a brilliant protégé of Bournonville), Pavel Gerdt, Nicholas Legat, or Enrico Cecchetti—four of the most technically accomplished dancers and teachers of the Russian ballet, men who are legendary today. Pavel Gerdt's career as the greatest classical danseur, partner, and mime of the period lasted an incredible fifty-six years, from 1860 to 1916, fifty of them as premier danseur on the Russian Imperial stage; he was the first Prince Siegfried in Petipa's *Swan Lake*. Nicholas Legat left Russia in 1914 to pursue his career as a teacher of Russian technique in the West; among his greatest students was the danseur André Eglevsky. The Italian dancer and ballet master Enrico Cecchetti won undying fame in his own right as a brilliant danseur as both the first Bluebird, a technically demanding *demi-caractère* role, and the first Carabosse, one of the most outstanding mime roles in all of ballet, in Petipa's *Sleeping Beauty;* he was also the teacher of such great dancers as Vaslav Nijinsky, Léonide Massine, Anna Pavlova, Alexandra Danilova, Alicia Markova, Anton Dolin, and Serge Lifar.

Much of the choreography for male dancing that was attributed to Petipa in his own time was actually set by his assistant, Lev Ivanov, a maligned and underrated artist. Petipa was French by birth, Russian only by adoption; at that time, Russia so admired France that it spoke French in its court, aped French manners, and copied French fashions. Ivanov, who was Russian-born, would probably have emerged as a much more important figure in nineteenth-century ballet had he not been subjected to the anti-Russian prejudice then in fashion. The male dancers, performing Ivanov's choreography, were the principal beneficiaries of his extraordinary talent. And it is to Ivanov that we owe one of the most familiar of all ballets, *The Nutcracker.*

Swan Lake, which Petipa choreographed with Ivanov, remains the standard of classical ballet. It is one of the touchstones of the ballerina's art, with its dual role of Odette, the gentle, enchanted swan maiden, and her evil impersonator, Odile; but in recent years it has become almost equally a vehicle for the danseur noble. Prince Siegfried is now called upon not only to partner the ballerina in her celebrated adagio in the second act and to perform as both partner and soloist in the Black Swan Pas de Deux in the third act; since Nureyev, it has become frequent practice to insert an adagio solo at the end of the first act, to display both the Prince's controlled elegance of line and his yearning, melancholy state of mind.

Erik Bruhn's and John Cranko's productions of *Swan Lake* make Siegfried the dramatic focus of the ballet. Bruhn's Siegfried, which he danced with the National Ballet of Canada in the latter years of his career as a danseur noble, is conceived as a young man trying to break away from the domination of his princess-mother, who has demanded, as in more traditional productions of the ballet, that he choose a bride. Bruhn goes on to emphasize Siegfried's mother-complex by presenting the Prince's evil genius as a woman, the Black Queen, rather than

as the customary sorcerer, von Rothbart, who has enchanted Odette and later tempts the hero with her simulacrum, Odile. Siegfried's choice between the White and Black Swans is presented in Bruhn's version as a choice—never to be revoked—between pure and physical love. Siegfried makes the wrong choice (of physical love, the Black Swan) and chooses to die rather than further betray his ideal.

John Cranko's version of *Swan Lake,* choreographed for the Stuttgart Ballet in 1963, was an attempt, in the choreographer's own words, to see that "the prince emerges as a living person who experiences a tragic ordeal, rather than being a human crane who simply lifts the ballerina. . . . Consider the situation: Siegfried proves unworthy, he breaks his vow and unconsciously confuses outward appearances with inner reality . . . he is a tragic hero and must be vanquished." There is no reunion in life, as in the Soviet version of the ballet, or in death for Cranko's lovers. Siegfried is drowned by von Rothbart in a stage storm in the tradition of *Götterdämmerung.*

Most productions of *Swan Lake* hew more closely to traditional lines of character interpretation, leaving it to individual exponents of the role to endow Prince Siegfried with more than a cardboard personality and to assert their own stage presence. Younger danseurs, who may be more than secure with the technical demands of the role, often seem uneasy with all the traditional princely standing about, receiving garlands and homage and "talking" in mime, especially in the first act; in the third act many danseurs avail themselves of the option of leaving the stage altogether during the national dances, as though bored with this court entertainment, returning only in time for the entrance of Odile and the ensuing pas de deux with her. Yet all of this *can* be performed with fascinating interpretive variations, as has been amply demonstrated by such different Siegfrieds as Rudolf Nureyev and Richard Cragun, the one a bored, almost neurotically melancholy aristocrat, the other virile and open.

At the heart of *Swan Lake* are the great pas de deux, and no danseur can possibly succeed in this ballet unless he is a strong cavalier for the ballerina. *Swan Lake* is almost the trademark for many of the most famous partnerships in ballet, such as Margot Fonteyn and Rudolf Nureyev, or Antoinette Sibley and Anthony Dowell of Britain's Royal Ballet. The Swan Queen can be only as good as her Siegfried, since we see her essentially from his perspective; the subtle changes that he must make in his performance to accommodate the dual Odette-Odile are often overlooked. Great dancers such as these, as Erik Bruhn has written, "can lift each other to a degree that neither could have reached without the other."

Until quite recently, the male dancer fared even less well in the other Petipa-Tchaikovsky masterpiece, *Sleeping Beauty,* often called the definitive statement of the classical ballet. The

Anthony Dowell as Solor with members of the Royal Ballet corps in Rudolf Nureyev's production of the Kingdom of the Shades, from La Bayadère.

story needs no retelling; it will be recalled that the Prince (variously called Florimund, Desire, or Charming, depending on whose production you see) awakens the sleeping princess with a kiss only at the very end of the fairy tale. Consequently, in the original and most subsequent versions of the ballet, the Prince does not even appear until the second act; he does not dance until the grand pas de deux with Princess Aurora in the last act. Attempts have been made to rectify this situation: Sir Frederick Ashton, for example, inserted a new pas de deux for Aurora and Florimund in the awakening scene of the Royal Ballet's 1968 production. But Rudolf Nureyev's staging of *Sleeping Beauty* for the National Ballet of Canada, with three variations for the Prince added in the second act, is perhaps the best-known version of the ballet with augmented choreography for the male. This does not mean that there is traditionally no male dancing in the ballet. The male star of the ballet was—and often still is—the strong technician who performs the *demi-caractère* role of the Bluebird in the last act, at Aurora's wedding celebration. The steps of batterie and elevation incorporated in the Bluebird's solo by Enrico Cecchetti, who created the role, are a continuing challenge to danseurs. Michael Coleman of the Royal Ballet, Vyacheslav Gordeyev of the Bolshoi, and Frank Augustyn of the National Ballet of Canada are outstanding Bluebirds of today.

Although Lev Ivanov, that comparative champion of male dancing, gave us the third of the Tchaikovsky ballets, *The Nutcracker,* it originally contained no outstanding performance opportunities for the danseur, apart from the one or two divertissements and the grand pas de deux in the second act. Today, these are variously assigned to the Sugar Plum Fairy and the Nutcracker Prince, as in Balanchine's version for the New York City Ballet, or to the Nutcracker Prince (as a dream manifestation of Herr Drosselemeyer) and Clara, the "little girl" heroine in Nureyev's stagings of the ballet who dreams of the Rat King and of her own adventures with the Nutcracker Prince.

It is impossible to discuss recent renderings of the Petipa classics without mentioning the name of Nureyev over and over again. The man is responsible for a great deal in contemporary ballet, including staging the first Western production of the last act of Petipa's *La Bayadère* in 1963 for the Royal Ballet, himself dancing the role of the warrior Solor who searches in the Kingdom of the Shades for his lost love, Nikiya (played by Margot Fonteyn). Nureyev's enormous vitality makes him a more aggressive Solor than, say, Britain's Anthony Dowell, a danseur noble whose elegant line and musicality make him a more traditional exponent of the role; there is no denying that Nureyev brings to Solor a dazzling presence that not only competes with his ballerina, but may even reduce her to a second-

ary presence at times. Natalia Makarova has staged a slightly different version (1974) of the Kingdom of the Shades for American Ballet Theatre, and when she performs the role of Nikiya, whether it be with Baryshnikov or Fernando Bujones or Ivan Nagy, the spotlight is on *her,* the ballerina; the ballerina was, after all, the focal point of Petipa's conception.

Raymonda and *Don Quixote* are two other full-length Petipa ballets that Nureyev has restaged in the West. Its highly melodic Alexander Glazounov score and Balanchine's choreography for his *Raymonda Variations* (revised as *Cortège Hongrois*) had kept the former ballet alive in the memory of European and American audiences, but it took Nureyev's elaborate, ambitious productions of the complete *Raymonda,* most recently for American Ballet Theatre, to give the ballet a new lease on life. With Nureyev in the augmented role of the Crusader Jean de Brienne, Cynthia Gregory in the title role, and Erik Bruhn as the "other man" in Raymonda's life (or dreams), the Saracen warrior Abderachman, the production opened to mixed reviews in New York in 1975. Nevertheless, it will probably remain in the repertoire as a unique vehicle for not one but two danseurs and an opportunity for audiences to compare two of their favorite male dancers in one performance.

Nureyev's *Don Quixote* is based loosely on the Kirov production, which is derived ultimately from Petipa's St. Petersburg version. The spirit of the original is preserved, while Nureyev once again provides himself (and danseurs to come) with a bravura role, that of the quicksilver, comic Basilio, the barber who is in love with Kitri, the innkeeper's daughter. Sir Robert Helpmann played the title role in the film version of Nureyev's production of *Don Quixote* for the Australian Ballet, in 1972.

Nureyev's desire to redefine the characterization in the Petipa formula is not an approach that he originated. For within Petipa's own lifetime, a rebellion was brewing. Many people felt that his works were stale, and his last ballet, *The Magic Mirror,* was deemed a disaster by the time of its premiere in 1903 at the Maryinsky Theatre. Waiting in the wings was a new generation that would repudiate the structure Petipa had built. It would reembrace the naturalistic principles of Noverre and carry the "new" Russian ballet to the West. Michel Fokine was the leading choreographer in this movement, but it was the extraordinarily gifted impresario Serge Diaghilev who would provide the vehicle, a company called the Ballets Russes. And the danseur who would become the crown jewel of this glittering array of Russian performers was the man who is still regarded as the greatest danseur in history, Vaslav Nijinsky. Brought up in the Petipa tradition, Nijinsky would leave Russia with Diaghilev, and his name would become synonymous with the highest excellence in ballet.

Opposite: The great dancer-actor Sir Robert Helpmann in the mime role of Don Quixote, with Ray Powell as Sancho Panza, in Rudolf Nureyev's production of Don Quixote *for the Australian Ballet.*

48

3

The Living Legend of Nijinsky

Nijinsky. The name brings to mind a standard of excellence for male dancers that has perhaps never been surpassed. Since his dazzling Paris debut in 1909, his name has become synonymous with the supreme expression of the art of ballet. The immediacy of the legend is even more extraordinary when one considers that few people alive today ever saw him dance, and there are no known films of him dancing. Our knowledge is garnered from photographs, first-hand accounts, and second-hand speculations. Of his performance in Fokine's *The Specter of the Rose,* it was said that he became "the very perfume of the rose." Jean Cocteau wrote of Nijinsky in that role: "His hands became the foliage of his gestures, and his face was radiant." His phenomenal elevation and technique were combined with an intuitive dramatic skill and a mesmerizing stage presence; today these qualities can only be imagined.

Nijinsky's life and accomplishments continue to provoke analysis and speculation, for as decisive as his contributions were—especially in restoring public interest in the male dancer—they were also shrouded in mystery. He has been called both an idiot and a genius, and it is clear that he appeared to his contemporaries as a mixture of both. That he was an idiot has never been proved, unless the reference is to a Dostoevskian kind of innocence. That he was a genius is also difficult to support, except that here we have the more tangible evidence of his ballets, which have earned for him a reputation as the first "modern" choreographer of the present century. Although his intellectual abilities have been hotly debated, he did possess a great gift of intuition, which he expressed in artistically innovative ways.

There have been and still are contenders to the Nijinsky legend—danseurs such as Massine, Dolin, Eglevsky, Nureyev, and Baryshnikov, among others—and yet the unique position that Nijinsky established for himself during his brief career has remained unshaken. That is in part because he startled the West into realizing that men could create beautiful movements in ballet. Nijinsky is associated particularly with two famous ballerinas, Anna Pavlova and Tamara Karsavina. But once Michel Fokine began to create roles for him, in ballets choreographed around a male protagonist, he was called upon to do very little traditional partnering. And as an actor and danseur capable of performing astonishing pyrotechnics, he was without peer. When dancing a role, he is said to have had an uncanny ability to assume the character so completely that he actually *became* the character. (This was both a gift and a curse, for when he was twenty-nine, he was hospitalized for schizophrenia.) Offstage, he was quiet, shy, and in possession of very few friends.

And yet this man, so painfully retiring, became enormously popular, and in the process advanced the popularity of ballet. Those who were drawn merely by curiosity at his renowned leaps and turns and his notorious animal magnetism stayed on to see the rest of the evening's performance—and came back again and again.

Nijinsky was the key element in Serge Diaghilev's stunning Ballets Russes. This troupe started as a group of Russian dancers on summer vacation from the Imperial Ballet; it turned into the seminal force in ballet in Europe and America during the period from 1909 to Diaghilev's death in 1929. Although Nijinsky's choreography is often overshadowed by the work of his contemporary Fokine, it is evident now how innovative his ballets were: Nijinsky not only strove for the heights—as in his airborne performances—he also explored the earthbound and the human, the explicitly sexual, particularly when he created his own ballets.

Amid the many fragments of Nijinsky's life, there is evidence that he was especially sensitive to the sorrows and annoyances common to all men. He nervously chewed and picked at his thumbs, sometimes until they became raw and bled. He was temperamental, growling at his ballerinas and threatening construction workers with a chair during rehearsals. His choreography was very difficult to perform, demanding

Preceding pages, left to right: *Nijinsky in great roles by Fokine that affected the course of modern ballet: The Specter of the Rose; the Favorite Slave in* Scheherazade; *Petrouchka.* Opposite: *Nijinsky in Fokine's* Le Pavillon d'Armide.

intense concentration and unending rehearsals in which the other dancers had to copy exactly what Nijinsky demonstrated but did not explain; he required an unprecedented number of rehearsals for his revolutionary *The Afternoon of a Faun,* the first ballet he choreographed, and he did not have enough rehearsal time for *Tyl Eulenspiegel,* his last. A riot broke out in the theater during the first performance of his most important ballet, *The Rite of Spring,* so startling were the innovations of both Nijinsky's primitive, earthbound choreography, with its turned-in feet, and the dissonance of Igor Stravinsky's score. To this day, there is still mystery surrounding Nijinsky's impromptu marriage in 1913 to a wealthy Hungarian woman who had single-mindedly followed him across continents and oceans, although he was probably the one man in Diaghilev's company who seemed most unlikely to marry. For it is generally known that Diaghilev was homosexual and was in love with Nijinsky; he clearly dominated Nijinsky for both personal and artistic ends. Nevertheless, Nijinsky, characteristically innocent, believed that Diaghilev would be delighted by the news of his marriage. Instead, Diaghilev fired him.

Nijinsky was swayed by Tolstoyism; he was interested in yoga; he was traumatized by the war. By the time he gave a last, pathetic concert in Switzerland shortly before his hospitalization, he had come to regard himself not only as a man of God, but literally as God himself.

Richard Buckle, author of the definitive biography *Nijinsky,* writes that "Nijinsky's life can be simply summarized: ten years growing; ten years learning; ten years dancing; thirty years in eclipse. Roughly sixty in all." Everything that Nijinsky did during his productive years had an impact. In his choreography he explored a wide range of experience and feelings, yet what he himself felt cannot be known for certain. His *Diary,* written just prior to his mental breakdown, gives a clue to his inner workings, but his enigmatic personality continues to stimulate comment, and his dancing still excites comparisons with contemporary performers.

Nijinsky was born in Kiev in 1888 into poverty, the son of Thomas Nijinsky and Eleonora Bereda, both Polish dancers from dancing families. He was the middle child of three: his older brother, Stanislav, was marked for a rather short and dismal lifetime, during most of which he was insane; his younger sister, Bronislava, became a dancer and choreographer in her own right, and her early career—like that of her famous brother's—was tied up with the fortunes of Diaghilev's Ballets Russes.

Thomas Nijinsky was something of a rake, and he eventually abandoned the family altogether, leaving his wife Eleonora to provide sole support for the children; she was relieved and

fortunate to find a place for her younger son, Vaslav, at the Imperial Ballet School in St. Petersburg, where he would be clothed, fed, trained, and boarded at the czar's expense. The child of generations of dancers, Nijinsky's physique was promising, and Nicholas Legat, one of his future teachers at the school, remarked at the time of his acceptance as a day student in 1897 on the peculiar musculature of his legs, which would be regarded as a factor in his ability to perform extraordinarily high, long leaps. Years later, Marie Rambert described this physical phenomenon in discussing Nijinsky in her autobiography *Quicksilver:*

> The most absurd theories were put forward about his anatomy. People said that the bones in his feet were like a bird's—as though a bird flew because of its feet! But, in fact, he *did* have exceptionally long Achilles tendons, which allowed him with his heels firmly on the ground and the back upright to bend the knees to the utmost before taking a spring, and he had powerful thighs.

But these were the observations of hindsight, based on the achievements of a mature artist. Many a child outgrows such early physical promise, and when Nijinsky began his studies, at the age of ten, only his vocation as a dancer was assured, both by the necessity of his mother's reduced circumstances and by his family's orientation toward the dance.

Nijinsky's early teachers were the famous Legat brothers, Sergei and Nicholas, who through their teacher, Christian Johansson, were schooled in the style of August Bournonville. And Bournonville was in turn a pupil of the great Vestris, with whom Nijinsky would be compared so often during his performing career. Others important to Nijinsky's early development included Pavel Gerdt, who had been the most famous danseur of his time; Anatole Oboukhov, a strong classicist who would eventually teach a later generation of dancers in New York City; and the famous danseur and mime Enrico Cecchetti, author of the Cecchetti system of training still in use today.

Nijinsky's school years were bedeviled with problems. His great talent manifested itself quite early, arousing the jealousy of his fellow students, who already scorned him for what they considered to be his "inferior" Polish ancestry. Nijinsky was also relatively inarticulate, a problem that would in later years result in slurs on his intelligence. An example of this is an anecdote, perhaps apocryphal, in which an amazed viewer asked of one of his effortless leaps in *The Specter of the Rose,* "How do you do it?"

"You have to just go up," he replied simply, "and then pause a little up there."

By 1902, Nijinsky was appearing in small parts in the Maryinsky Theatre, which was closely connected with the ballet school. The repertoire of the company was made up primarily of classical Petipa fare, but objections to the rigid format of

Opposite top left: *Adolf Bolm in Fokine's original choreography (1909) for the* Polovetsian Dances *from* Prince Igor. *Opposite top right: Anthony Dowell in Nijinsky's role in* Les Sylphides. *Opposite bottom: The Moiseyev production of the* Polovetsian Dances.

these works were beginning to be heard. A few progressive choreographers such as Fokine were seeking more expressive ways of dancing, in line with the teachings of Noverre and Stanislavsky, but they were having a difficult time with the ballet company's administration, which was extremely conservative. This artistic conflict would eventually cause a schism within the Maryinsky. The Imperial Ballet's loss would provide Serge Diaghilev with the talent he needed to form his first Ballets Russes.

In 1907, Nijinsky, then nineteen years old, was chosen by Russia's prima ballerina assoluta, Mathilda Kchessinska, to part-ner her in a series of performances—an almost unheard-of honor for so young and inexperienced a dancer. That same year, the night before his official graduation from the Imperial Ballet School, Nijinsky created the role of Armide's slave in Fokine's first ballet for the Maryinsky Theatre, *Le Pavillon d'Armide*. His relationship with Fokine was to have great significance in the years to come, for Fokine, the most important choreographer of the early twentieth century, choreographed the roles in *Les Sylphides, Scheherazade, The Specter of the Rose, Petrouchka,* and other ballets that will forever be associated with Nijinsky.

Fokine's rebellion against the academic limitations imposed on ballet during Petipa's regime at the Maryinsky Theatre led to his formulation of principles that were to revolutionize ballet in the West. Fokine dethroned the ballerina in his ballets, giving equal if not greater importance to the danseur and to the corps de ballet; his choreography demanded expressivity and musicality in movement, rather than dazzling technique. In his ballets, he attempted a true fusion of choreographic concept, music, and design.

Before Isadora Duncan, the great exponent of "natural" dance, ever visited Russia, Fokine had choreographed *The Dying Swan;* a solo piece made famous by Anna Pavlova, it established a new fluidity of movement in ballet, made possible because the ballerina's torso was freed of the heavily boned bodice that had been the standard costume. Fokine went on to use such techniques to even greater effect in his choreography for *Les Sylphides* in 1908; within the framework of that neo-Romantic ballet blanc he asked his dancers (among them Pavlova, Karsavina, and Nijinsky) to respond to the Chopin score with ecstasy, in a style of movement that freed their upper torsos, arms, and heads from the rigid classical positions of *port de bras.* In fact, though Nijinsky's interpretive gifts were great,

Nijinsky in the Danses Siamoises divertissement from Fokine's Les Orientales, *which was premiered in 1910, the same year as* Scheherazade. *The exoticism of these ballets influenced the popular fashions and decor of the time.*

57

he owed the wide range of his roles largely to Fokine's creative genius—from the lyrical poet of *Les Sylphides* to the turned-in, tragic figure of Petrouchka to the airborne Specter of the Rose. Fokine in turn must have been greatly inspired by Nijinsky's gifts. Yet neither of these great artists might ever have been known in the West, or have reached the full fruition of his talents, had it not been for Serge Diaghilev.

As a young dancer at the Maryinsky, Nijinsky had little time for social activity. The free time he did have, between daily class, rehearsals, and performances, was spent primarily among people connected with the czar's court. It was through one of these, Prince Pavel Dmitrievitch Lvov, that he was introduced in 1908 to Serge Diaghilev, an impresario who during this period was engaged in taking Russian art and opera to Paris.

Nijinsky's subsequent relationship with Diaghilev was characterized by the older man's complete dominance over the younger. Diaghilev's role in their liaison was that of the father Nijinsky had never really known; and he provided the young dancer with material comforts he had not previously enjoyed. To his credit, Diaghilev managed to make Nijinsky's name a household word and provided a steady performance base for his exceptional dancing.

Diaghilev's mission was to take Russian art to the West. As a musician, editor, and writer, he had met with little success; as a cultivated man, his ability to discover unknown talent and to propel his closest associates into experimentation was to change the face of ballet, bringing both dance and music fully into the twentieth century. He was forever seeking the new, the astonishing, the different. His company of choreographers and dancers liberated ballet from the strictures of Petipa classicism, and he brought about an increasingly unified (and exotic) blend of scenic elements with music and dancing. Even his programming altered the traditional format: instead of one evening-long ballet, he presented three or four works, of varying styles.

Diaghilev's "moderns" included composers Igor Stravinsky, Maurice Ravel, Claude Debussy, and Richard Strauss—all of whom provided scores for Nijinsky's choreography—as well as Sergei Prokofiev, Francis Poulenc, and Erik Satie; among his choreographers, in addition to Fokine and Nijinsky, were counted Léonide Massine, Bronislava Nijinska, Serge Lifar, and George Balanchine. His list of designers was no less impressive—he and Jean Cocteau later sparred over which one of them had first discovered Picasso. His dancers included nearly two generations of performers, since his company became, in its time, the only serious stronghold of ballet in the West.

In 1907, Diaghilev arranged for an exhibition of Russian paintings in Paris, the first such exhibit ever held. In 1908, he took the Russian Opera from the Maryinsky to Paris, introducing the great bass Fedor Chaliapin to the West in the title role of *Boris Godunov.* That year also marked the introduction of Nijinsky to Diaghilev, who was preparing to organize a company of Russian dancers to perform in Paris the next June.

Nijinsky had been performing during the season of 1907–1908 with the ranking ballerinas of the Maryinsky, and Fokine had set his neo-Romantic ballet *Chopiniana* for a charity performance in St. Petersburg with Nijinsky in the lone male role. Later revised as *Les Sylphides,* the ballet is almost a cliché on the stage today, often a parody of its former self; the freedom from classical restraint that Fokine envisaged for his dancers has frozen into the kind of ritual reverence often accorded a great work of art. Then too, the role created by Nijinsky is notoriously difficult to duplicate; he brought an androgynous quality to the role, as a young man inspired and intoxicated by the music and by his partners. Cyril Beaumont, in *The Diaghilev Ballet in London,* describes "the billowing of his white silk sleeve as he curved and extended his arm; then that lovely movement when, on extending his leg in a *développé,* his hand swept gracefully from thigh to shin in a movement so graceful and so delicate as to suggest a caress." With all its intangible qualities, *Les Sylphides* was the first "abstract" ballet and was revolutionary for its time. It has been much copied over the years and is retained in the repertoires of most major companies; danseurs such as Erik Bruhn, Anthony Dowell, and Ivan Nagy have performed Nijinsky's role to critical acclaim.

In 1909, Diaghilev's Ballets Russes made its first appearances in Paris, with *Les Sylphides* included in its repertoire, and the Parisian audience was driven wild by the revelation of Russian male dancing. The first ballet on opening night was a reworking of Fokine's *Le Pavillon d'Armide,* an eerie tale of witchery and enchantment. Nijinsky danced the role of Armide's Favorite Slave, for which he wore a costume reminiscent of those worn by male dancers in the eighteenth century. The atmosphere in the audience was electric, and, responding to this, Nijinsky leaped offstage rather than walking off after the pas de trois that followed his solo variation. The gasps were audible throughout the house, for Parisian audiences had not seen such virtuosity as Nijinsky's since the time of Vestris. On the same program, Diaghilev presented the second act of the opera *Prince Igor,* with the virile danseur Adolph Bolm leading a corps de ballet of Russian character dancers in Fokine's breathtaking *Polovetsian Dances.* Nijinsky appeared again in *Le Festin,* the series of Petipa divertissements that closed the program. Members of the audience stormed the stage after the performance and crowded around the dressing rooms to get glimpses of the new stars, who found themselves unexpectedly the toast of Paris.

The second ballet program, presented two weeks later, included *Les Sylphides* and Fokine's *Cleopatra,* an exotic work

Nijinsky and Tamara Karsavina in Act II of Diaghilev's 1911 Giselle. *During his years with the Ballets Russes, Nijinsky was often paired with Karsavina.*

Nijinsky was not only a virtuoso dancer with incomparable
elevation and ballon—he was a brilliant dancer-actor as well.
Petrouchka, the anguished puppet, was his greatest
role. The ballet has been staged countless times since the
original 1911 production by the Ballets Russes, and many
danseurs have essayed the title role. But it is said that
no one has equaled Nijinsky's performance. Above:
Christian Holder as the Blackamoor, Susan Magno as the
Ballerina, and Gary Chryst as Petrouchka in the first scene
of The Joffrey Ballet production. The three puppets have
been brought to life by the Old Showman (Basil Thompson)
to dance for the crowd at the St. Petersburg fair. Right:
Mikhail Baryshnikov as Petrouchka, with William Carter of
American Ballet Theatre as the Showman. Opposite left:
Studies of Nijinsky (top) and Nureyev (bottom) as
Petrouchka. Opposite top right: Nureyev as Petrouchka is
stunned by the Blackamoor's jealous blow. Opposite bottom
right: Chryst as the dying Petrouchka appeals for help and
understanding from the crowd.

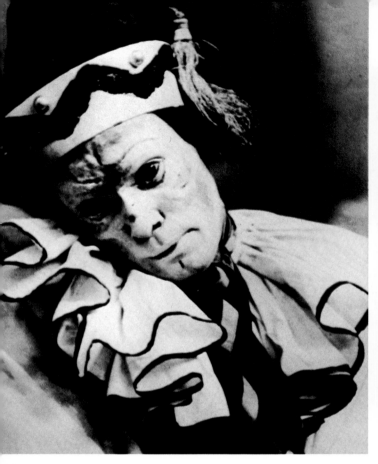

with costumes and decor by the great designer Léon Bakst, in which Nijinsky had the relatively minor role of one of Cleopatra's slaves. These ballets were as well received as those on opening night, and subsequent performances by the company were sold out. In one season, Diaghilev and his dancers—particularly Nijinsky and Bolm—had gone a long way toward reestablishing the vital role of the danseur; Diaghilev and his artistic collaborators, Alexandre Benois, Léon Bakst, and Fokine, had reaffirmed ballet as a major art form.

The Ballets Russes returned to Paris in 1910 with several works for Tamara Karsavina and Nijinsky added to its repertoire. Fokine staged a production of *Giselle* (which had not been seen in Paris since 1868), both as a gesture to the appreciative French audience and as a vehicle for the two leading dancers of the company. But although Nijinsky agonized over his dramatic interpretation of Albrecht, seeking to reduce the formal mime and to incorporate the more natural style of dance-acting that he had been absorbing in his association with Fokine, the ballet still seemed old-fashioned and rather dull to the Parisians. They applauded Karsavina and Nijinsky—who had succeeded at least in restoring dramatic perspective to the role of Albrecht, as well as thrilling them with his dancing in the second act—but they reserved their real enthusiasm for the new works that Diaghilev brought them that year. Nijinsky was to have his real triumph in Fokine's *Scheherazade.*

Scheherazade was more than an attempt by Diaghilev to capitalize on his previous success with the exotic *Cleopatra;* it marked the fusion of concept, design, music, and choreography that had been Fokine's and Diaghilev's expressed aim for many years. Its story was fitted to already existing music by Rimsky-Korsakov; Bakst's hitherto unheard-of color combinations for elaborate costumes and opulent decor (peacock blues and greens, tomato red) became the rage of the design world, influencing both fashion and the decorative arts. And Fokine's choreography—not only for Nijinsky as the Favorite Slave, but also for Zobeide, portrayed by the great mime actress Ida Rubinstein, and for the corps de ballet—has been hailed as a masterpiece for its time.

"Savage . . . a stallion" (Fokine); "a flame of lust . . . a devil" (Geoffrey Whitworth); "half cat, half-snake, fiendishly agile, feminine and yet wholly terrifying" (Benois)—these are descriptions of Nijinsky's mesmerizing performance as the leaping, sensuous Favorite Slave. This was the virtuoso Nijinsky, totally immersed in a role at the opposite end of the spectrum from the graceful poet of *Les Sylphides;* he made his entrance in a leap that was "like an arrow from a bow, in a mighty parabola which enabled him to cross in one bound a good two-thirds of the width of the stage" (Cyril Beaumont, *The Diaghilev Ballet in London*). And thence from orgy to massacre, when Zobeide and the harem are discovered by the King

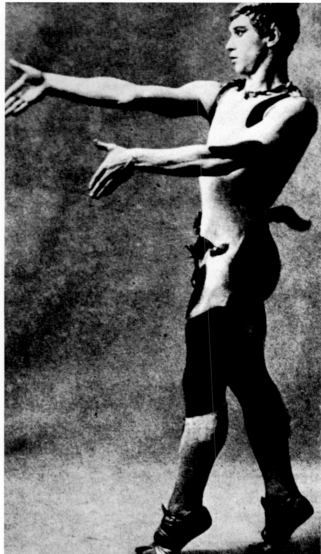

with their slaves. It was shocking, it was wild; but because of the high level of creative collaboration, it was art. Diaghilev had discovered the *succès de scandale,* and his adherence to this principle was to keep his company riding the crest of popularity for years to come.

The Ballets Russes of 1910 was still a company that functioned only in the summertime, when the dancers were on leave from regular positions with the Maryinsky in St. Petersburg. But an event took place in 1911 that helped make it possible for Diaghilev to realize his dream of a year-round company: his most important dancer, Nijinsky, was summarily dismissed from the service of the Maryinsky Theatre for wearing what the authorities considered an improper costume during a performance of *Giselle.* Albrecht's traditional costume included a pair of shorts, which contemporary standards of modesty decreed

should be worn over his tights; Nijinsky had omitted the shorts. Whether he had been urged to this misbehavior by Diaghilev has been disputed; but the effect of his hasty dismissal was to deprive Russia of Nijinsky's dancing for the rest of his career. Nijinsky left Russia that year, and although he had no such intention at the time, he was never to return to his homeland.

The success of Karsavina in Stravinsky's *Firebird* in 1911 had determined Diaghilev to commission for Nijinsky an equally important protagonist's role. The collaboration of Fokine, Stravinsky, and Benois on *Petrouchka* was the result.

Petrouchka is redolent with the flavor of early nineteenth-century Russia. It is set at a winter carnival, during the last week before Lent, in a public square in St. Petersburg. An element of mystery is introduced into the general scene of merrymaking in the person of a magician, who produces three wonderful, life-

Opposite: *Antoinette Sibley and Anthony Dowell in Jerome Robbins's modern rendition of* The Afternoon of a Faun, *a work originally created by Nijinsky.*
Above: *Two views of Nijinsky in his original version of the ballet.*

63

danseurs who have essayed the title role includes Léonide Massine, Leon Woizikowski, John Kriza, Jerome Robbins, and Borge Ralov; Nureyev, Bruhn, and Baryshnikov are among those performing Petrouchka today, as is The Joffrey's brilliant young character dancer, Gary Chryst. But those who saw Nijinsky claim that he has never been equalled in the part; only *he* is the immortal Petrouchka, the indomitable spirit of the oppressed.

Nijinsky's life at this time was running a curious parallel to his puppet role; Diaghilev, the showman, was pulling all the strings, but Nijinsky was growing restless. In 1912, at Diaghilev's insistence that he try his wings as a choreographer, Nijinsky created his first ballet, the controversial *The Afternoon*

size puppets. These are Petrouchka, a sad-faced clown; a pert Ballerina; and a Blackamoor. Petrouchka is in love with the Ballerina, but she spurns him in favor of the Blackamoor. In the final scene, set in the midst of the carnival, the Blackamoor chases the broken-hearted Petrouchka and murders him with his scimitar. As the onlookers leave the square, the indomitable spirit of Petrouchka is seen crying out in anguish from a rooftop —a spokesman for all who are enraged and frustrated by life.

Once again, Fokine's choreography used only those movements that he felt were appropriate to his theme. Petrouchka's whole bearing is limp, turned in; his hands, those extremities of a dancer's line, are blunted, encased in mittens; for Nijinsky in this role there were to be no virtuoso displays. But Nijinsky was no mere technician of the dance. Stravinsky tells us: "To call Nijinsky a dancer is not enough, for he was an even greater dramatic actor. His face could become the most powerful actor's mask I have ever seen and, as Petrouchka, he was the most exciting human being I have ever seen on a stage."

That 1911 season also saw Nijinsky's first performance as the mischievous Harlequin in Fokine's *Le Carnaval* as well as the premiere of *The Specter of the Rose,* but Petrouchka was his greatest role, as it was the supreme achievement of Fokine and a landmark in musical and ballet history. *Petrouchka* has been performed in scores of productions around the world since its premiere, notably in recent years by the Royal Ballet, The Joffrey Ballet, and American Ballet Theatre. The list of

Top: *Baryshnikov is one of many contemporary danseurs to dance the role created for Nijinsky in Fokine's* The Specter of the Rose. *Above:* Nijinsky during his first Paris season. *Opposite:* Nijinsky with Tamara Karsavina in *Specter.*

of a Faun. Although Diaghilev and his associates would later take credit for Nijinsky's work on this and other ballets, there is sufficient evidence to indicate that Nijinsky's genius found its most natural outlet in choreography. There is no denying the fact that, at the peak of his career as a dancer, Nijinsky chose, not to create a ballet that would display his abilities as a danseur, or even as an actor, but to choreograph an experimental work of great difficulty that explored new possibilities of movement. The question often raised, of whether Nijinsky's choreographic contributions exceeded his role as a danseur, cannot be satisfactorily answered, but if he was a great choreographer, then he, with Stravinsky and Picasso, was one of the makers of the modern movement that was to bring the arts fully into the twentieth century.

The Afternoon of a Faun is set in ancient Greece. Alone at first, the Faun (danced by Nijinsky in a revealing, close-fitting costume of patterned one-piece tights) soon encounters a group of seven nymphs, who are repelled by the beast and hurry away. One of the nymphs, in her haste, leaves behind a scarf, which the Faun seizes and caresses. The movement that so startled the audience in Paris in 1912 may seem rather tame to theatergoers today: the Faun takes the scarf, lies down with it upon a rock, and makes a very subtle masturbatory gesture. At

Nijinsky with his wife, Romola, and their daughter, Kyra.

the premiere, the audience went wild with mingled enthusiasm and disapproval, and Diaghilev ordered the ballet repeated so that the evening could continue. The police were present for the next performance, and the offending gesture was slightly modified—so slightly that even those who had seen it before could not tell the difference; but the theater was not closed.

If being so explicit sexually was something of a first in this ballet, there were other, more important factors discernible from today's liberated perspective. The dancers were directed to disregard the five basic positions of classical ballet and to perform instead highly stylized friezelike movements. The entire work was performed with the face and feet in profile, while the torso and arms were presented flat to the audience. As a measure of the difficulty of this new ballet, its twelve minutes of dancing required a total of 125 rehearsals (about three months' time), 90 of which were needed to retrain the classically based dancers in Nijinsky's new technique.

The ballet caused great controversy in the press, but no less a personage than the sculptor Auguste Rodin came to Nijinsky's defense. He wrote to the papers that

> Nijinsky possesses the distinct advantage of physical perfection, harmony of proportions, and a most extraordinary power to bend his body so as to interpret the most diverse sentiments . . . in no part is Nijinsky as marvelous as in *The Afternoon of a Faun.* No jumps, no bounds, nothing but attitudes and gestures of a half-conscious creature. He stretches himself and retreats, with movement now slow, now jerky, nervous, angular; his eyes spy, his arms extend, his hands open and close, his head turns away and turns back. . . . His whole body expresses what his mind dictates. He possesses the beauty of the antique frescoes and statues; he is the ideal model for whom every painter and sculptor has longed.

The Afternoon of a Faun is the only ballet by Nijinsky that has survived, though it is performed only rarely today, more as a choreographic curiosity than as a repertoire piece. The original version has been supplanted by Jerome Robbins's modern treatment of the Debussy score, in which a young danseur, alone in a ballet studio, stretches and examines himself in an imaginary mirror. He is joined by a young danseuse; they dance together; he kisses her cheek; she departs. A narcissistic, coolly sensual young man and a modern nymph—the kiss and the girl's departure are a faint echo of the sexual implications in Nijinsky's ballet.

Nijinsky clearly identified with the half man, half beast he had created in his work, and in later years he would write in his *Diary,* "I am the Faun." The *Faun* expresses an awakening longing in one of nature's creatures for members of the opposite sex. Diaghilev seems to have missed the importance of this point—had he not done so, it would certainly have given him cause for concern, if not alarm.

Nijinsky's success was, of course, also Diaghilev's. Diaghilev felt that the future of the Ballets Russes lay with the development of his prodigy. This resulted in misunderstandings with Fokine, who was still the company's principal choreographer, and shortly after *Faun*'s premiere, Fokine left the company; though he returned briefly the following year, this was the beginning of his final break with Diaghilev. This loss, for which Diaghilev's machinations were partly to blame, placed a burden of responsibility on the shoulders of Nijinsky. Now, more than ever, he had to succeed.

Nijinsky's second work for Diaghilev, *Jeux*, choreographed to a commissioned score by Debussy in 1913, was a further attempt to explore new movement possibilities. Although it has gone down in dance history as one of the first ballets with a contemporary setting—a tennis match—it was doomed to failure at the time of its creation. Once again, Nijinsky's behavior during rehearsals led to tremendous friction with his dancers, who received little help from him in understanding the concept of the work; indeed, Nijinsky himself was hampered by the necessary transposition of the ballet's slight plot, from a story of three young men to a story of the ambiguous relationship among one young man and two girls. And the sports metaphor that he had been given by Diaghilev as part of his ''modern'' theme was unfortunate, because Nijinsky knew next to nothing about popular sports—his supposed tennis gestures were more reminiscent of golf! *Jeux* lasted only a few performances and then was lost; it was quickly overshadowed by the dynamic primitivism of *The Rite of Spring*, which is regarded as Nijinsky's masterwork.

The genesis of *The Rite of Spring*, which also received its premiere performance in the 1913 season, is an interesting and well-documented collaboration. Igor Stravinsky and the designer Nicholas Roerich originally conceived the ballet (to Stravinsky's score) as plotless, danced only by a corps de ballet, which would perform dances based on classical technique. But the technique that Nijinsky created for this work was like none Parisians had ever seen. A plot was added that dealt with the ritual sacrifice of a virgin to assuage the mysterious powers of the god of light during the awakening of a ''violent Russian spring,'' as Stravinsky called it. The time of the story was thrust back to prehistory, to an age when men were inchoate savages —and Nijinsky, the man who had mastered an airborne style of dancing for himself, created choreography that suggested the movements of earthbound beasts that seemed barely able to stand. The central role—the Chosen Virgin, who is forced to dance herself to death—was said to be the most difficult role ever created for a woman, in part because the dancing was based on turned-in feet rather than the classically turned-out positions. Undoing the years of classical training and grasping

Nijinsky's new technique was nearly impossible for the dancers of that period.

To many who saw it, *The Rite of Spring* appeared ugly, the movements obscene and antidance; but its defenders recognized it as an important advance in twentieth-century ballet. There was nearly a riot in the theater at its premiere, and the screaming and stamping during the first performance were so deafening that the dancers could not hear the music. Nijinsky, standing in the wings (he did not dance in the ballet), had to pound out the complicated rhythms with his fists so that the dancers might continue. Critically, the ballet attracted considerable attention, and the packed houses on succeeding nights of its performance were less unruly as people began to appreciate the primitive beauty and the propelling, rhythmic force of the work. Nijinsky and Stravinsky, as a result, were hailed as the two leading exponents of modernism—the one in dance, the other in music.

Ironically, nothing of Nijinsky's choreography remains, although the basic elements of anticlassicism were retained in later versions of the ballet set to the same score. A 1920 version by Massine was given in collaboration with Martha Graham in Philadelphia in 1930, which is all the more complimentary to Nijinsky's daring innovation because Graham had already de-

Nijinsky in Jeux, *with Karsavina (left) and Schollar.*

Opposite: *Mikhail Baryshnikov is supported by Clark Tippett and Charles Ward of American Ballet Theatre in Glen Tetley's version of* The Rite of Spring. *The original version, choreographed by Nijinsky in 1913 for Diaghilev's company, was the subject of scandal; unfortunately, the choreography has been lost.* Right: *Jorge Donn as Nijinsky in Maurice Béjart's* Nijinsky, Clown of God, *which deals with the dilemmas and great roles that were part of the Russian danseur's life. The enormous puppet in the background represents Diaghilev, the impresario who was a major force in starting Nijinsky on his spectacular though short-lived international career as a dancer.*

clared her "war" on ballet. Maurice Béjart, whose fascination with Nijinsky found its fullest expression in his epic work *Nijinsky, Clown of God,* choreographed a version of *The Rite of Spring* in 1959 that looks very much the way Nijinsky's ballet has been described; Glen Tetley, who choreographed the ballet in 1974, has transposed the role of the sacrificial victim to a male dancer.

Through all of this, Nijinsky had become an artist secure with his talent, and this security seems to have reduced his dependence on Diaghilev. He spoke more freely in public, expressing ideas of his own; he began to regard Diaghilev's constant involvement in his life as oppressive and intolerable.

Diaghilev's Achilles' heel proved to be his superstitious fear, prompted by a fortune-teller, that he would die at sea (in fact, he did die *by* the sea, in Venice in 1929); because of this, he bypassed the opportunity to travel with his company on a tour to South America. Nijinsky, the star of the company, went on the twenty-two-day boat trip, a free man for the first time in years. By the time the ship docked at their destination, he had become engaged to a very determined young woman named Romola de Pulszky, who came from a prominent Hungarian family. The courtship must have been one of the strangest on record, for neither Vaslav nor Romola could speak a language known to the other, and Nijinsky's sudden proposal came as an unexpected shock even to the adoring and aggressive girl—who was on the voyage for no other reason but this. Vaslav and Romola were married in Buenos Aires on September 10, 1913, to the consternation and wonderment of everyone in the company. Diaghilev was slow to react to the news, but when he did, his reply to the danseur's declaration of independence was curt and to the point. Nijinsky received a telegram that read: "Your

services with the Russian Ballet are no longer required. Do not join us. Serge de Diaghilev." Privately, to the designer Léon Bakst, Diaghilev declared, "As high as Nijinsky stands now, so low am I going to thrust him," a vengeance that was made much easier by the young danseur's increasingly unstable mental condition.

Nijinsky made several attempts to function on his own. After word of his dismissal leaked out, he was besieged with offers, and he attempted to stage his own eight-week season in London at the Palace Theatre, a vaudeville house that he mistakenly believed was parallel in prestige to the renowned Covent Garden. He had to sandwich his dancing in among other acts, and the entire experience was a disaster, financially as well as artistically.

Romola gave birth to the first of two daughters, Kyra, and the outbreak of the First World War found them staying with Romola's family in Hungary, where Nijinsky, still a Russian citizen, was arrested and interned as an enemy alien. Technically he was now a prisoner of war, and he was forbidden to leave his in-laws' home, where Romola's family was openly hostile to him. During this dismal period, he was not even allowed to rehearse, and the lethal combination of enforced inactivity and uncertain prospects seems to have aggravated the process of mental deterioration.

Several attempts had been made by mutual friends to effect a reconciliation between Nijinsky and Diaghilev, whose company was scheduled to make its first American tour with the provision that Diaghilev—who made the fearful voyage this time to oversee his obligations—come with the dancers about whom America had been reading since 1909, especially Nijinsky. Through diplomatic channels, the American impresario

Otto Kahn managed to arrange for Nijinsky's release, and Vaslav, Romola, and their baby daughter arrived in New York in the spring of 1916. They were to remain in America, performing and traveling, for almost a year.

Nijinsky wanted to perform for the Americans, who had arranged for his release, but his relationship with Diaghilev was seldom less than tense. In his *Diary,* Nijinsky wrote both that he loathed Diaghilev and that he was deeply indebted to him as well. During that first New York season, Nijinsky became the darling of society, performing his familiar roles in *The Specter of the Rose, Scheherazade,* and *Petrouchka.* At a tableau vivant given by Mrs. William K. Vanderbilt, he appeared in costume—only to find out afterward that his underwear had been stolen by society women. He had never signed a contract with Diaghilev in the early years of their association, and in fact had been forced to sue for his back salary; but he was now making the astronomical salary of $3,000 a week. Diaghilev openly expressed the opinion that this fee was too high.

After the first tour to New York was over, the company returned to Europe, leaving the Nijinskys to spend the summer in the States, during which time Nijinsky prepared his new ballet, *Tyl Eulenspiegel,* for its premiere in New York the next fall. Otto Kahn insisted that Nijinsky and not Diaghilev supervise the second tour, and the strain of that responsibility took its toll on the dancer.

Tyl Eulenspiegel seemed to be unusually ill-fated. The strong anti-German sentiments in America during the war prejudiced people against the Richard Strauss score. Instead of six weeks' rehearsal, Nijinsky had only three, with young and somewhat inexperienced dancers provided by Diaghilev. Having choreographed himself in the leading role of the medieval prankster, Tyl, he sprained his ankle and should not have danced at all—but did, with considerable pain. He was shorthanded administratively, which was compounded by his having made some ill-advised managerial decisions. According to some reports by the dancers, he was becoming extremely difficult to work with—vague, withdrawn, and given to tantrums. He believed himself the victim of malicious plots; his dancing seemed to suffer as well, some said. But several people who had known him well, including the danseur Adolph Bolm and the writer Carl van Vechten, said that he had never danced better. Despite the hardships, the critical response to the new ballet was quite favorable, and it seemed to win the admiration of its audiences. It was performed during the four-week cross-country tour that followed the New York premiere—and then it was dropped forever.

The overall success of *Tyl Eulenspiegel* proves that Nijinsky at that time was capable of creating a full-length ballet in his own style without the supervision of Diaghilev. It serves as a reply to those who have challenged the authorship of Nijinsky's work. If there was a plot against Nijinsky, it was one to discredit him in the hope that credit rightfully belonging to him would be transferred to the Ballets Russes, which would never again achieve the luster it had had when Nijinsky was its principal performer and choreographer. Although his association with the company continued intermittently until his last public performance, in September of 1917 in Buenos Aires, his increasing isolation from the ballet world eventually resulted in the mental breakdown from which he never fully recovered. Nijinsky grew more and more withdrawn; he hallucinated; he walked through a small Swiss village wearing a large gold cross, asking strangers if they had been to Mass. In St. Moritz in 1918, he gave a private recital for 200 invited guests; he danced only after spending an interminable amount of time sitting and staring

at his audience. Romola describes the scene in her biography of her husband:

> Vaslav was dancing—gloriously but frighteningly. He took a few rolls of black and white velvet and made a big cross the length of the room. He stood at the head of it with open arms, a living cross himself. 'Now I will dance you the war, with its suffering, with its destruction, with its death. The war which you did not prevent and so you are responsible for.' It was terrifying. . . . He seemed to fill the room with horror-stricken suffering humanity. It was tragic; his gestures were all monumental, and he entranced us so that we almost saw him floating over corpses. The public sat breathlessly horrified and strangely fascinated . . . and he was dancing,, dancing on. Whirling through space, taking his audience away with him to war, to destruction, facing suffering and horror, struggling with all his steellike muscles, his agility, his lightning quickness, his ethereal being, to escape the inevitable end. It was the dance for life, against death.

This was the last performance by the danseur of *Les Syl-phides, Scheherazade, The Afternoon of a Faun, The Specter of the Rose;* it was perhaps closest in its pathos to *Petrouchka.* If Nijinsky was incoherent on this occasion, if his audience was shocked by what it witnessed, it was not the first time that he had been misunderstood. This was Nijinsky, speaking the language in which he was most fluent, soul to soul, trying to say with his body what his mind refused to articulate in words. He was ahead of his time; this kind of personal, visceral expression was for many years to be the province of modern dance, and not the ballet stage. If his mind had not been clouded by schizophrenia, what might not Nijinsky have achieved?

The legend of the dancer lives; the choreography provokes fresh analysis of its daring experimentation; the *Diary* of his tortured spirit is still read.

Nijinsky gave his last performance in 1918.

He died in 1950.

A religious man in real life, Nijinsky is represented as being overwhelmed by moral and religious conflict in Béjart's ballet Nijinsky, Clown of God. *Here, Jorge Donn dances the title role.*

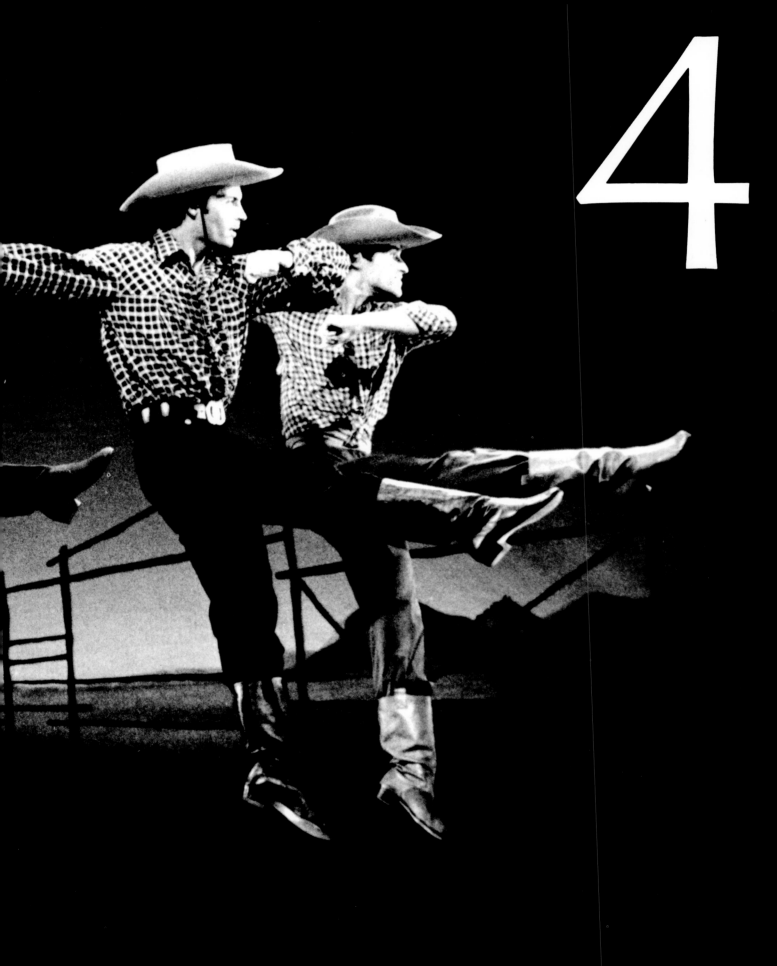

4

Princes and Pas de Deux: The Heirs of Diaghilev

In Fokine and Nijinsky, Diaghilev had brought two of the seminal figures of twentieth-century ballet to the attention of the West. The fortunes of the male dancer continued to intertwine with Diaghilev's Ballets Russes after Nijinsky's dismissal in 1913 and Fokine's departure in 1914. In addition to his personal inclination, Diaghilev realized that another male star of Nijinsky's stature would have great box-office appeal. While on a visit to Russia, he saw the young actor-dancer Léonide Massine; recognizing potential greatness in the handsome, dark-eyed young man, he invited him to join his company.

Whereas Nijinsky had had an established career in Russia before he ever met Diaghilev, Massine became a great dancer and choreographer almost entirely under Diaghilev's guidance. Massine had studied ballet at the Imperial School and worked with the Bolshoi, but at the age of seventeen, when he met Diaghilev, he was considering a career as an actor. Diaghilev offered him another kind of education: an opportunity to learn all the theater arts, not only from himself but from the greatest artists of the time, to whom Diaghilev had access—men such as Igor Stravinsky, Pablo Picasso, and Jean Cocteau.

With the special classical training by Cecchetti that Diaghilev provided, Massine triumphed as a dancer, and by the end of 1915, he made his debut as a choreographer with *The Midnight Sun*. Diaghilev was delighted, for he felt that by fostering Massine's creative talents he had found the perfect new instrument to express his own ideas about dance. In 1917, Massine astonished not only the Parisian public but his mentor with his ballet *Parade*. The result of a collaboration with Picasso (who designed the Cubist costumes and decor), Cocteau (who provided the theme), and Erik Satie (who wrote the score), *Parade* has been hailed as enduringly avant-garde, the first multi-media ballet. Massine was proving himself not only prolific, but controversial as well, the next in the Diaghilev chain of dancers, choreographers, and artists who would spread the Russian-preserved art of ballet from Russia to all of the world.

Massine made his name with Diaghilev—and quickly broke away. In 1921, with the success of *The Good-Humored Ladies, The Fantastic Toyshop,* and *The Three-Cornered Hat* behind him, he left the Ballets Russes to try his own wings. He was not only a dancer who needed to be provided with a steady stream of roles to perform—as all dancers do—he had become one of the major choreographers of the young twentieth century. In ballets such as *The Three-Cornered Hat,* for which he carefully studied the art of Spanish dance, he created vehicles for himself as a character dancer that would last for his long career. He was seldom surpassed in these roles.

Into the breach in the Ballets Russes created by Massine's defection stepped "Patrickieff." Diaghilev's company had been so successful in identifying the art of ballet as Russian that any dancer wishing to be taken seriously was forced to "russify" his or her name. Thus a young Englishman, Sydney Francis Patrick Chippendall Healey-Kay, was dubbed "Patrickieff" by Diaghilev when he was discovered in London in 1921; but the name he is remembered by is his second alias, Anton Dolin.

Dolin's training was of the catch-as-catch-can variety then available in England, although his studies with Serafina Astafieva, a former Maryinsky dancer who had opened a school in London, gave him the benefit of a St. Petersburg-style training. Dolin had had some early stage experience acting in plays and Christmas pantomimes; and this gave him a sure grounding in stagecraft.

Diaghilev saw Dolin at Astafieva's and cast him in the corps de ballet for the revival of *Sleeping Beauty,* which he produced in London in 1921; in 1923, he invited the young danseur to become a full-fledged member of the Ballets Russes. In one of several autobiographies, full of marvelous anecdotes, Dolin describes his early years with the company: his struggles to learn French and to cope with the exotic new environment in Monte Carlo; his classes with Bronislava Nijinska, Nijinsky's sister, who was then the company's ballet mistress; and his

Preceding pages: *The Joffrey Ballet in Agnes de Mille's* Rodeo.
Opposite top left: *Massine in Fokine's* The Legend of Joseph.
Opposite top right: *Massine as the Chinese Conjuror in his* Parade.
Opposite bottom: *Massine (right) with Diaghilev.*

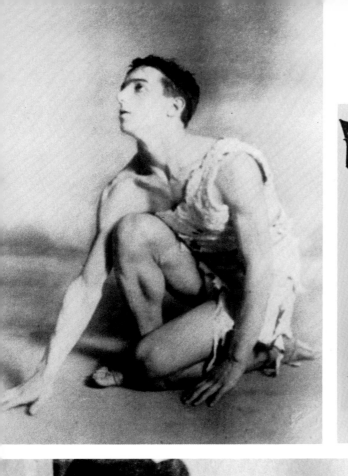

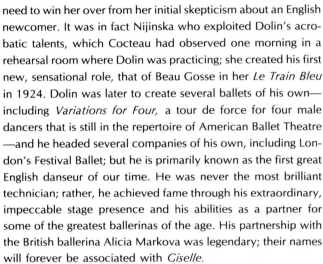

need to win her over from her initial skepticism about an English newcomer. It was in fact Nijinska who exploited Dolin's acrobatic talents, which Cocteau had observed one morning in a rehearsal room where Dolin was practicing; she created his first new, sensational role, that of Beau Gosse in her *Le Train Bleu* in 1924. Dolin was later to create several ballets of his own—including *Variations for Four,* a tour de force for four male dancers that is still in the repertoire of American Ballet Theatre—and he headed several companies of his own, including London's Festival Ballet; but he is primarily known as the first great English danseur of our time. He was never the most brilliant technician; rather, he achieved fame through his extraordinary, impeccable stage presence and his abilities as a partner for some of the greatest ballerinas of the age. His partnership with the British ballerina Alicia Markova was legendary; their names will forever be associated with *Giselle.*

Dolin's contemporary, Serge Lifar, on the other hand, was to achieve not only fame but a measure of notoriety in his long career. Born in Kiev in 1905, Lifar's first glimpses of dance were the folk dancing of Russian and Ukrainian soldiers. One day, a friend brought him to Nijinska's ballet studio in Kiev, and there Lifar found his lifework, though he was late in beginning it. After only a few years of determined study, Lifar was one of five dancers from Kiev to flee the Soviet Union in 1923 and join the corps de ballet of the Ballets Russes. In short order, in spite of his rudimentary training in ballet, his dark good looks and splendid physique caused him to be singled out by Diaghilev; he was the last dance protégé in the impresario's distinguished career.

The verdict of history has been mixed on Lifar's achievements, both as dancer and as choreographer. By 1925, after special tutelage with Cecchetti, he had replaced Anton Dolin as Diaghilev's premier danseur; and in 1928 and 1929 he was the first interpreter of the leading roles in two of the most important twentieth-century ballets for the danseur, both by George Ba-

lanchine, one of Diaghilev's most recent choreographic discoveries from Russia: his neoclassical *Apollo* and his superb dramatic ballet *The Prodigal Son.* Apart from their importance in Balanchine's canon, these roles are associated with some of the major danseurs of the century: Apollo with André Eglevsky, Jacques d'Amboise, Peter Martins, Edward Villella, and Rudolf Nureyev; the Prodigal Son with Jerome Robbins, Villella, and Nureyev. That Lifar scored a triumph in the premieres of these ballets is as much a tribute to his own gifts as to Balanchine's. Though some critics have not thought well of him, dance historians such as Lillian Moore and Cyril Beaumont have hailed Lifar as the heir to Nijinsky, praising his elevation and batterie and noting his ability to perform triple *tours en l'air.*

Lifar's other claim to a place in dance history stems from his years as director of and choreographer for the Paris Opera, an institution that had fallen into serious decline since the Romantic age, but that Lifar brought back to health. If the ballets he created—such as *Icare, Bacchus et Ariadne* and *Le Roi Nu*—were more vehicles for his own talents than immortal masterworks, they were nevertheless successful and popular in their time, and the principles of choreography enunciated by Lifar—that dance could be divorced from music, for example—were quite advanced, and in some cases suggested the directions taken by modern dance. But in his determination to be the savior of French dance, Lifar was accused of collaboration with the Nazis, during the Occupation in World War II. With the Liberation in 1944, Lifar was banned from French stages, but two years later, fully exonerated, he returned in triumph to the Paris Opera, to continue his work of restoring performance standards to the heights achieved during the Romantic period. Among the dancers who studied at the Paris Opera and began their careers there under Lifar's tenure were Roland Petit and Jean Babilée. Petit—a dynamic dancer and choreographer who went on to form several companies of his own—has created

Léonide Massine's Parade *in rehearsal and performance.* **Opposite left:** *Gary Chryst of The Joffrey Ballet receives instruction in the facial expressions of the Chinese Conjuror from choreographer Massine, who originated the role in 1917, while Robert Joffrey and members of the cast listen.* **Opposite right:** *Massine recreates his original makeup for Chryst, while Claude Picasso, son of the ballet's designer, records the moment.* **Left:** *Chryst performs the Chinese Conjuror's solo in a faithful replica of the brilliant and colorful costume by Picasso, which made the Conjuror for a time the logo for Diaghilev's Ballets Russes.*

many dramatic ballets, including *Carmen* (1949) and *Le Jeune Homme et la Mort* (1949). The latter work, with its theme by Cocteau of a young artist lured to death by his lover, may be considered the archetype of French postwar ballet; it was a famous vehicle for the intense stage presence and dazzling technique of Babilée. The role of the Young Man has recently been essayed by both Nureyev and Baryshnikov.

With the death of Diaghilev in 1929, Lifar was among many who were cast adrift in an uncertain dance world. For twenty years, the Ballets Russes had represented the best in dance to audiences both in Europe and in America; it had been the haven and the goal of the greatest dancers of its time. Other companies, such as Rolf de Maré's avant-garde Ballets Suédois, flashed across the scene like comets and disappeared; Pavlova's world tours were made with pick-up companies selected as settings for the great ballerina. Outside of Denmark and Russia, there were no national companies of repute, no schools to provide dancers for the future. It was a precarious time for ballet, an art form that one forgetful generation could destroy, since there was still no generally accepted way of recording choreography; yet anyone who would step into Diaghilev's shoes must be brave—or foolhardy—indeed.

Lifar found his niche with the Paris Opera Ballet in 1930; for Dolin, Massine, Balanchine, and the others cast adrift from the steady performing base that Diaghilev had provided, the next decade would be peripatetic and perpetually insecure. None of the companies that attempted to recreate the formula of the Ballets Russes during this period was entirely successful, and there was much legal wrangling over which impresario had the right to use the name Ballets Russes, as well as much switching of positions among the creative personnel. Yet the thirties, for all their historic confusion and backstage rivalry, were an incredibly fertile period for dance, dancers, and the growth of

Above: *Massine as the Peruvian in his own* Gaieté Parisienne. Opposite: *Anton Dolin and Leon Woizikowski in Bronislava Nijinska's 1924 ballet* Le Train Bleu, *a work that exploited Dolin's considerable acrobatic talents.*

Opposite top: *Serge Lifar, Diaghilev's last protégé, in his own ballet* Icare. *Opposite bottom:* Alicia Alonso *and* André Eglevsky—*a great danseur of the '30s, '40s, and '50s—in Balanchine's* Apollo. *Below, from left to right:* Karin von Aroldingen, Suzanne Farrell, *and* Gloria Govrin *as the three Muses and* Peter Martins *in the title role of* Apollo *at Balanchine's New York City Ballet.*

George Balanchine's Prodigal Son, *created in 1929 for Diaghilev's Ballets Russes with Lifar in the title role, was revived by the New York City Ballet in 1950 with Jerome Robbins as the Prodigal. In recent years, the danseur most often associated with this technically demanding dramatic ballet has been Edward Villella, of the New York City Ballet.* Top: *Villella as the Prodigal Son falls in with evil companions.* Above: *At the conclusion, he begs forgiveness from his father.* Opposite: *His defiant leap on leaving home at the start of the ballet.*

public enthusiasm for ballet. Few works from this period survive on the stage today, but the foundations were laid, especially in Britain and in America, for schools and companies of international caliber that are now among the greatest in the world.

Ballet during the thirties was still basically European-Russian, and most of the male stars of the various manifestations of the Ballets Russes—Youskevitch, Eglevsky, Franklin, and others—were the products of an Old World heritage.

Igor Youskevitch, born in Russia in 1912, was one of the great technicians and danseurs nobles from the late 1930s till the 1950s. His family fled Russia during the Revolution, and Youskevitch grew up in Yugoslavia. It was there, early in 1932, that he began his studies; and only two months after they started, he embarked on his career as a dancer, partnering Yugoslavian dancer Xenia Grunt in a series of concerts. If the duration of his training seems impossibly brief, it becomes more believable in the light of his athletic prowess as a teenager in track, swimming, and gymnastics, in which he won many awards. Athletics had developed his strength and coordination to a high degree, and his musicality was enforced by a method of training that involved working at sports to the strains of waltzes and other dance rhythms.

Nevertheless, two months of study, however intensive, are hardly sufficient training, and it soon became necessary for Youskevitch to make the decision of his life: to move to Paris, where he could work with Olga Preobrajenska and other fine teachers who had settled there. Within a few years he was performing as a soloist in Colonel de Basil's Ballets Russes; in 1938, he followed Massine to the Ballet Russe de Monte Carlo, where he became a principal dancer.

In the 1930s, Massine created some of the most talked-about and daring ballets of his career: not only such cheerful and popular diversions as *Le Beau Danube* (a revision of an earlier work) and *Gaieté Parisienne,* but his ambitious and controversial symphonic ballets set to the music of composers such as Shostakovitch, Brahms, and Berlioz. In his *Gaieté Parisienne,* Massine danced the role of the Peruvian who visits a Paris nightclub at the turn of the century; Youskevitch created the part of the Young Officer. Youskevitch also first interpreted the roles of the Man in White in *Rouge et Noir* (set to Shostakovitch's First Symphony) and Mercury in *Seventh Symphony* (set to the music of Beethoven).

But Youskevitch is principally remembered for his brilliant, virile classicism and his partnership with the Cuban ballerina Alicia Alonso in ballets such as *Giselle* and Balanchine's *Theme and Variations.* Youskevitch, who had visited America with the Ballet Russe de Monte Carlo, returned during the Second World War, joined the American Navy, and became a citizen; until 1962, when he retired, he made his career as the most distin-

guished danseur noble of his generation in the United States.

André Eglevsky, Youskevitch's compatriot and near contemporary (he was born in 1917), had an equally distinguished career—not only in Europe but in America, which was increasingly the setting for major events and careers in the international world of ballet. Eglevsky's family, too, had emigrated from Russia during the Revolution, settling in Nice. There Eglevsky, a frail child of eight, was sent to study ballet with Maria Nevelska, in hopes of improving his health. Nevelska claimed that she soon recognized his potential as a danseur, and when Michel Fokine confirmed her judgment, in response to an application from the anxious Madame Eglevsky, the boy's profession was decided upon.

Like Fernando Bujones today, who has been hailed since his teens as a dance prodigy, Eglevsky was a *wunderkind* of his generation. In 1936, he performed Nijinsky's roles in *Les Sylphides* and *The Specter of the Rose,* rehearsing both ballets with Fokine himself. The following year the British critic Richard Buckle wrote of the already famous young star: "At the age of nineteen he possesses an almost perfect technique and a fine sense of mime."

Eglevsky became an American citizen in 1939 and appeared with a number of companies, primarily in America, during the forties and fifties. Some of his most fruitful years as an artist were spent with American Ballet Theatre (1942–1943 and 1945), where he created the role of Paris in Fokine's posthumous ballet *Helen of Troy* and danced in Balanchine's *Apollo* and all roles associated with the classical cavalier; and with the New York City Ballet (1951–1958), where Balanchine created his *Pas de Trois* (to Minkus), giving Eglevsky the chance to display his brilliant ballon and batterie. With the American ballerina Maria Tallchief, he enjoyed a notable partnership during the years he spent with the New York City Ballet, and they appeared together in many Balanchine works, including *Scotch Symphony.* Like Youskevitch, who appeared in Gene Kelly's all-dance film *Invitation to the Dance,* Eglevsky made a foray into cinema with his performance with Melissa Hayden in Charles Chaplin's *Limelight* in 1952. Both danseurs, now retired, are passing on their art as teachers, each having founded a school and his own semiprofessional company.

Freddie Franklin may not seem a very prepossessing sort of name after all the Slavic syllables to which the Ballets Russes had accustomed its public. But Freddie Franklin, born in 1914 in Liverpool, once one of the Lancashire Lads (a music hall "turn" that introduced Franklin to Paris, Josephine Baker, and Mistinguette), became the Frederic Franklin whose charm of personality as a dancer was compared to that of his fellow Englishman Cary Grant as an actor. Franklin claims to have known at the age of four that he wanted to be a dancer, but

ballet training and opportunities to perform classical dance were not easily come by in Britain in the early thirties, and Franklin did a stint in musical comedy.

In 1932, Franklin met Wendy Toye, a sixteen-year-old British dancer who was enjoying extraordinary success in shows and supper clubs, and the two began a partnership that was to rekindle Franklin's interest in ballet and bring him to the notice of Anton Dolin, to whom Franklin gives credit for his own emergence as a ballet star. Studies with Dolin, Nicholas Legat, and others strengthened and polished Franklin's technique, and in 1935, Dolin gave him the chance to join the recently formed Markova-Dolin Company as a soloist. Touring with these two great dancers and their troupe for two years, Franklin performed many of Dolin's own roles in ballets such as Nijinska's *Les Biches* and Fokine's *Carnaval* (in which the role of Harlequin had been danced by Nijinsky as well). In 1938, the company disbanded, and Franklin accepted Massine's invitation to join the Ballet Russe de Monte Carlo. It was here that he created most of the roles for which he is chiefly remembered as a danseur: his romantically serious Baron in *Gaieté Parisienne,* single-mindedly pursuing Alexandra Danilova, the fickle Glove-Seller; his noble portrayal of the Spirit of Creation in Massine's *Seventh Symphony.* But Franklin was known not only for his performance of the classics and particularly for his partnership with Danilova in ballets such as *Coppélia.* With his stage charm and his English name—which made him seem less exotic and perhaps more suited to such roles—he was the first Champion Roper in Agnes de Mille's *Rodeo,* the first to play the title role in Ruth Page's *Billy Sunday,* and with his own company, the Slavenska-Franklin Ballet, the first to essay the part of Stanley in Valerie Bettis's ballet version of *A Streetcar Named Desire.*

In addition to his performing abilities, Franklin found himself blessed with a memory for detail and a flair for conveying style and teaching technique—the marks of a fine ballet master. Balanchine recommended him for this important post with the Ballet Russe de Monte Carlo, and he was given it in 1944. He has long since made his permanent home in America and was the director of Washington's National Ballet from its inception in 1962 until its demise in 1974. As teacher, he provides an invaluable link to a vital period in ballet history, to works and performance styles that otherwise might be lost. But no one is ever likely to call Freddie Franklin a grand old man of the dance. He remains witty and accessible, and can even be lured back to the stage from time to time to perform roles such as Dr. Coppelius, investing his portrayals with the richness of detail that is the heritage of his lifetime in the theater.

The tours of the Ballets Russes companies brought Youskevitch, Eglevsky, and Franklin to the United States—not only

Lew Christensen was one of the most important American danseurs of the '30s to perform both classical roles and ballets with American themes. He is seen here as Mac, the filling station attendant, in his own 1938 ballet Filling Station.

to perform, but ultimately to stay, even beyond the war years that had made European touring for these companies unfeasible. They found an audience in America that was not only receptive to the best that they and the "Russian" ballet had to offer, but was also increasingly enthusiastic about native experiments. These experiments were being made by companies such as The American Ballet, founded by Balanchine and Lincoln Kirstein in 1934 and the first incarnation of what is now the New York City Ballet; Ballet Caravan, which joined with the American Ballet in 1941 under the new name American Ballet Caravan; and Ballet Theatre, now known as American Ballet Theatre. Ballets like Lew Christensen's *Filling Station* (1938) and Eugene Loring's *Billy the Kid* (1938), the latter with a superb score by Aaron Copland—ballets with American themes, created by American artists—required strong male protagonists. That need was filled by American danseurs such as Lew Christensen, considered by many to have been America's first premier danseur, and John Kriza, who became closely associated with the title role of *Billy the Kid* in the Ballet Theatre revival. Christensen, a young blond Danish-American, had a background in vaudeville in an act with his brothers Willam and Harold; his entire family, in fact, had been involved in music and dance for several generations. He came out of Utah to become the first American Apollo in Balanchine's premiere production of this ballet in the United States. If it still imported much of its glamor from abroad, ballet in America was coming of age, finding its own themes and rhythms and performing personalities.

Loring's *Billy the Kid* and Agnes de Mille's *Rodeo* (1942) focused on the legend of the American West, using Western manners and folk material in movement idioms that expressed the open stance of the cowboy. Their work suggested horses being ridden in wide-open spaces, pioneer spirit, elementary emotions. In a different vein, another American dancer, twenty-five-year-old Jerome Robbins, choreographed his first ballet, *Fancy Free,* in 1944. Working with composer Leonard ·Bernstein on a jazzy score, he chose for his theme three sailors on shore leave and created a vignette of life in New York City. A talented, dramatic dancer, who performed roles ranging from Petrouchka and the Prodigal Son to parts in some of his own ballets, Robbins himself danced the role of the sailor with the Latin rhythm, while John Kriza played the romantic and Harold Lang the virtuoso. *Fancy Free* was so successful in its fusion of ballet with jazz and popular dances, so true to the spirit of its time, that it launched Robbins on a career in the musical theater, doing the choreography for *On the Town, West Side Story,* and *Fiddler on the Roof,* among other hits (just as de Mille's *Rodeo* had led to her choreography for Broadway, most notably to *Oklahoma!*). In fact, Robbins's career alternated for some

years between ballet and the Broadway stage; now he seems to have found his home as a choreographer and ballet master of the New York City Ballet.

George Balanchine's New York City Ballet can scarcely be thought of as the repository of ballet's greatest roles for the danseur—Balanchine's well-known predilection for the ballerina and for feminine performance qualities has expressed itself again and again. Yet the company has not altogether slighted the danseur, and Balanchine ballets from *Apollo* to *Orpheus* to *Agon* have provided splendid opportunities for the male.

In fact, it was Balanchine and Lincoln Kirstein, his partner in the founding of the New York City Ballet, who were responsible for giving Arthur Mitchell, America's first great black classical dancer, a career in ballet. Mitchell had been a child of Harlem, a scholarship student in modern dance at the High School of the Performing Arts in New York, and had no thought of entering the white world of ballet until Kirstein put the idea in his head and challenged him to make the dream come true. He had no desire to be taken into the New York City Ballet as a token black, so he tried and worked harder—and entered the company as a principal in 1955, as a replacement in *Western Symphony* for Jacques d'Amboise, who was making a film in Hollywood. Mitchell's pantherine grace and stage charisma in roles created for him by Balanchine—including Puck in *A Midsummer Night's Dream,* a focal pas de deux in *Agon* with Allegra Kent, and the revised *Slaughter on Tenth Avenue* ballet, which he danced to sensational effect with Suzanne Farrell—ensured his success as one of the company's leading danseurs, the first black in the history of ballet to achieve such a position with a major classical company. Blessed with seemingly boundless energy, as well as talent, he had several simultaneous careers, as a star of the New York City Ballet, as a performer in musical comedy, as a teacher, and as director of Brazil's first ballet company; after the initial period of organization, he "commuted" to Brazil to fulfill his obligations there.

But with the assassination of Martin Luther King in 1968, Mitchell's life became focused on one goal: the establishment of a school in Harlem for black students of ballet and, subsequently, of a company in which the best of them could perform. His standards, set by Balanchine and Kirstein, were high. Buoyed by their faith and substantial help in matters of repertoire and fund raising, as well as by the new administrative confidence he had gained after the success of his Brazilian venture, Mitchell began laying plans for the Dance Theatre of Harlem in 1968, and the company made its official debut in 1971. Black dancers who had joined companies in Europe and regional companies in the United States flocked to join, and the company has now fulfilled a large portion of its initial promise.

Top: Eglevsky as Paris in the Fokine-Lichine ballet Helen of Troy. *Left: Igor Youskevitch and Alicia Alonso in Balanchine's* Theme and Variations. *Above: Jean Babilée and Nathalie Phillipart in Petit's* Le Jeune Homme et la Mort.

87

While Mitchell is pleased to give these professional dancers performing opportunities they might have been denied elsewhere, he is particularly thrilled by the enthusiasm, the will to succeed, and the sheer talent he finds in the black children whom he exposes to dance—almost seizing them off the street, it has been said. Mitchell has effectively counteracted a long-standing prejudice against blacks in ballet; he has proved with his body, his style, and his eclectic interest in many forms of dance that a black in ballet can be beautiful.

The "Russian" ballet—no longer really Russian, as it had long since been infiltrated by dancers from the West—was more or less stranded in the United States during the Second World War, and here it became more and more Americanized. But there was yet another influence on American dance and dancers to be accounted for: the British. America had adopted Frederic Franklin; Dolin and Markova were the legendary partnership of Ballet Theatre, the stars who could routinely sell out the house; but Antony Tudor, the British choreographer who emigrated to America in 1939 with Hugh Laing, the danseur who performed some of his greatest works, profoundly influenced the course of ballet in the United States.

Opposite: *Alexandra Danilova and British danseur Frederic Franklin, as the Glove-Seller and the Officer, in Massine's effervescent* Gaieté Parisienne. *Left:* John Kriza *in the title role of Eugene Loring's* Billy the Kid. *Choreographed in 1938 for Ballet Caravan, this was one of the earliest ballets with an American theme, an American choreographer, and an American score (by Aaron Copland). It is in the current repertoire of American Ballet Theatre and the San Francisco Ballet. Below:* Mia Slavenska *as Blanche and Franklin as Stanley in Valerie Bettis's ballet* A Streetcar Named Desire *(1952), based on the Tennessee Williams play.*

Tudor was a nineteen-year-old clerk in London when he saw his first ballet performance and decided on a career in dance. But London in 1929 was not the thriving dance center that it is today. There were visits from Diaghilev and Pavlova, and the 1930s saw the Ballets Russes companies playing to sold-out houses in the West End, but other dance activity was scattered and small-scale. The future preeminence of the Royal Ballet was as yet a gleam in Ninette de Valois's eye. Meanwhile, a former Diaghilev dancer named Marie Rambert, of Polish origin, was presenting young dancers and choreographers of her own discovery on the postage-stamp stage of the Mercury Theatre in Kensington. It was to Rambert that Tudor went for training in ballet.

Tudor was never a great dancer, for his late start limited his personal technique. As a result, his ballets are concerned less with virtuoso display than with intimate gesture and probings of the heart and mind. Extremely musical and quick to absorb the rudiments of ballet training and put them to creative use, Tudor was choreographing ballets for Rambert just a few years after she engaged him as a kind of Jack-of-all-trades for her Ballet Club—he was secretary, rehearsal pianist, and janitor, all to support his studies and full-time obsession with ballet. From the beginning, his works nearly always included a role for his friend Hugh Laing, a darkly handsome, temperamental native of Barbados who came to London to study art and discovered himself as a dancer instead. While they were both with Rambert, Tudor choreographed two of his most enduring works: *Lilac Garden* (1936), with Laing as the lover of a girl who is forced into an arranged marriage with a man she does not love (portrayed by Tudor himself), and *Dark Elegies* (1937), an evocation of grief set to Mahler's *Kindertotenlieder*. Both of these ballets "traveled" well, and quickly established Tudor's reputation as a major choreographer when he restaged them in America for Ballet Theatre.

Although Laing danced in other ballets, he is primarily associated with the Tudor repertoire, which has been one of Ballet Theatre's crowning glories almost since its inception as the "museum" of the best in international ballet. *Pillar of Fire* was a famous vehicle for America's dramatic ballerina Nora Kaye, but Laing's sensual portrayal of The Young Man from the House Opposite was a chilling vignette; his Romeo to Alicia Markova's Juliet in Tudor's treatment of the story (with a score by Frederick Delius) was another memorable performance. In *Undertow* Laing became the protagonist, a psychopathic young man called The Transgressor who ultimately commits murder. In these ballets Tudor explored the psychology and emotions of real people—quite a new preoccupation when *Lilac Garden* was premiered in 1936—and he may be credited with extending the dramatic possibilities of the art.

With its Western theme, its happy ending, and its brilliant score by Aaron Copland, Agnes de Mille's **Rodeo** has been a popular success since first performed in 1942 by the Ballet Russe de Monte Carlo. Her choreography captured the open stance of the cowboy and a sense of the vast spaces and potential loneliness of the American Southwest, as well as the vigor of its people. Its subject was not the only element new to ballet: there were also the costumes—blue jeans and gingham—and a virtuoso tap solo, with which Frederic Franklin as the Champion Roper won the heart of the ballet's heroine, the Cowgirl (danced by de Mille herself). Dancers from The Joffrey Ballet are seen here in rehearsal and performance of the company's recent revival of the original production. *Opposite top:* Ballet master Paul Sutherland (right) rehearses the cowboys. *Opposite center:* The cowboys in action in the ballet's finale.
Opposite bottom: The Head Wrangler (Dermot Burke) loses the Cowgirl (Beatriz Rodriguez) to the kiss of the Champion Roper (Gregory Huffman). *Left:* Beatriz Rodriguez and Gregory Huffman at the Saturday night dance that ends the ballet. *Below:* Russell Sultzbach as the Champion Roper in the famous tap dance.

Since the forties, Tudor has produced little equal to his early work, although in 1967 he was apparently inspired by another great danseur, the Royal Ballet's Anthony Dowell, to create his rather mysterious *Shadowplay*. The ballet's theme is taken loosely from Kipling's Mowgli stories in *The Jungle Book*, colored by Tudor's long interest in Zen. Because of Tudor's association with American Ballet Theatre, *Shadowplay* has entered its repertoire, and The Boy with Matted Hair has been performed by both Baryshnikov and Fernando Bujones.

When Tudor and Laing left England in 1939, the country was on the brink of balletic greatness. Rambert's experiments at the Mercury had produced yet another choreographic genius in Frederick Ashton; and Ninette de Valois had seized on him to help her by creating a splendid repertoire for Britain's emerging national ballet, then called the Sadler's Wells and later the Royal Ballet. Before the war took the best of her young danseurs into the service, her company included Robert Helpmann, Harold Turner, and Michael Somes (in addition to the great ballerina Margot Fonteyn).

Turner was Britain's first virtuoso technician, initiating the tour de force of the whirling Blue Skater in Ashton's *Les Patineurs*. And Helpmann was the dramatic mainstay of the young Sadler's Wells company in the thirties and early forties, excelling particularly in character roles that made use of his dramatic flair. Born in Australia in 1909, Helpmann was encouraged to a theatrical career by his mother and had his first glimpse of ballet at a performance given by Anna Pavlova. He was enchanted; it was no longer enough to become an actor or even a Fancy Dancer—he must learn ballet. Forthwith he joined the Pavlova company on its Australian tour, taking daily lessons with Laurent Novikov, who was Pavlova's partner at that time.

In England, meanwhile, Pavlova's peripatetic touring had inspired yet another genius of the British ballet: Frederick Ashton, who had seen her dance with her company when he was a child in Peru. From then on, he was seized with the urge to dance—a horrifying prospect to his middle-class family, but one that he persisted in, secretly taking lessons from Massine (who told him to appear at his first class in soft shoes and pajamas!) and botching his job as a sort of foreign correspondent for a London business firm.

By the early thirties, Ashton was meeting with modest success as a choreographer for Rambert and de Valois. Helpmann had had his first major role as a dancer in de Valois's *Job* in 1933, and in 1936, he created the role of the Poet in *Apparitions*, which Ashton choreographed for Margot Fonteyn. (That ballerina was a major source of inspiration for Ashton's choreography throughout his career, and Helpmann was her regular partner until after the war.)

Helpmann's dramatic flair was evident in all his roles: as

Satan in *Job,* he was commandingly malevolent; as the doomed Master of Tregennis he dominated de Valois's *The Haunted Ballroom;* and of his Poet in the Ashton work it was said that "He excels above all, in the intimate detailed portraiture of the poet-aesthete, with his melancholy and sensuously gentle temperament. He has perfected a magical mood of bewitched and bewitching weariness."

Since Helpmann was another late starter in ballet, his technique left something to be desired. Nevertheless, he was soon proving himself not only in character roles, in which he was increasingly the master of brilliant make-up effects, but in classical roles such as Albrecht and Siegfried, which he danced opposite Fonteyn. In *Sleeping Beauty,* he combined the two branches of his danseur's skill, appearing both as the evil miming Carabosse and as Prince Florimund in the Sadler's Wells prewar production. With the war years, however, his versatility would prove indispensable to the company.

The army was calling up promising dancers like Michael Somes, until there was scarcely a man in the company old enough—or young enough—to support a ballerina. Ashton, the fountainhead of the repertory, was called up too, but the troupe continued to perform throughout the war under the most deprived conditions, for the sake not only of its art but for public morale. Helpmann was pressed into another kind of service, becoming a choreographer with his first ballet, *Comus,* and staging *Hamlet,* his most famous work. His version, inspired by the line "For in that sleep of death what dreams may come?" tells the story of Hamlet in flashback, beginning with the hero's body being borne from the stage by Fortinbras's captains. Thereafter, the Gravedigger, Ophelia, the Queen, and others are seen

Opposite top: *Arthur Mitchell rehearsing two young dancers from his Dance Theatre of Harlem.* Opposite bottom: *A younger Mitchell with Allegra Kent in Balanchine's* Agon, *created in 1957 for the New York City Ballet.* Above: *Jerome Robbins as a sailor in his first ballet,* Fancy Free; *it was also his first collaboration with Leonard Bernstein, with whom he would later work in musical theater.* Left: *Nicholas Magallanes, creator of the title role in Balanchine's* Orpheus.

in quick-melting sequences conjured up in Hamlet's brain. At the end, Hamlet is borne again from the stage, and the spotlight on his face goes out.

It was certainly theatrical; perhaps even, as one American critic claimed, "exaggerated pantomime" and scarcely dance. Helpmann himself in later years stated that he had had an ulterior motive in producing the ballet: that of convincing the Old Vic that he could play Hamlet as an actor—which he later did in Stratford. Nevertheless, controversial though it may have been, the ballet was a success and further established Helpmann as an actor-dancer without peer.

Helpmann was a unique performer in his alternation between the ballet and the dramatic stage for a good part of his career. He appeared also in speaking roles in several films, including that milestone in ballet history, *The Red Shoes,* for which he supplied the choreography as well. In 1965, he returned to his native Australia to head that country's national ballet with Dame Peggy van Praagh. Though he retired from this position in 1976, he is perhaps not yet immune to the smell of greasepaint. In recent years he has made brilliant comic character appearances in such ballets as Ashton's *A Wedding Bouquet* and in Nureyev's production of *Don Quixote* for the Australian Ballet.

Acting in dance was an attribute particularly associated with British ballet in the forties. The repertoire was made up largely of "story" ballets, a heritage perhaps of Britain's rich literary and dramatic history. The classics of dance—*Swan Lake, Giselle, Sleeping Beauty*—were much performed and revered, their romantic fantasy providing escape from the grim reality of the war years. Quintessentially English ballets such as *Job* and *The Rake's Progress* were inspired, respectively, by William Blake's etchings on the Biblical theme of Job's trials and by William Hogarth's eighteenth-century satirical drawings. Although each contained strong dance roles rooted in classical technique—Satan in *Job,* the precise Dancing Master in *Rake*—they were actually more pantomimic tableaux than ballets. If male dancers were scarce, male virtuosos were even scarcer. With little input from abroad during the war years, British dance and dancers had to learn to flourish on their own.

But once the war was over, Britain had—and still has—a relative abundance of character dancers. Chief among them was New Zealand-born Alexander Grant, who came to London after the war to study and quickly found himself performing principal roles. Stocky, sturdily built, and lacking the long, elegant line necessary for a danseur in princely parts, Grant excelled in the character repertoire during his long career with the Royal Ballet, and he must be ranked with Margot Fonteyn as one of the primary interpreters of Ashton's choreography, having created (and inspired) some twenty roles in Ashton ballets.

94

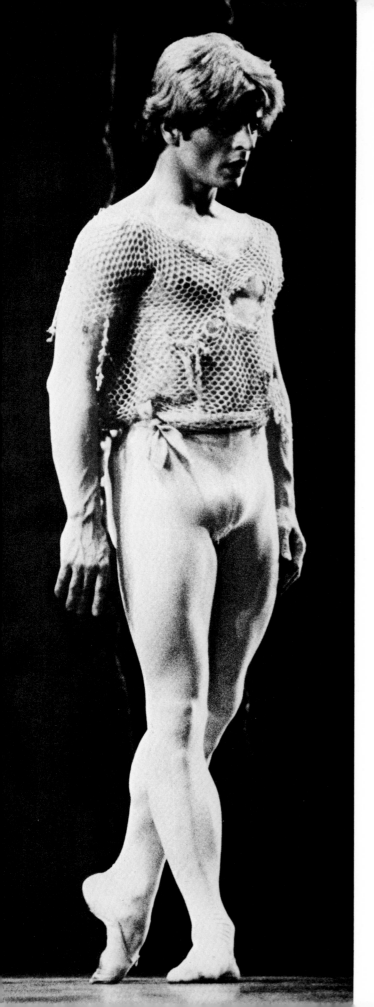

Opposite top: *George Balanchine rehearsing Arthur Mitchell in his ballet* Slaughter on Tenth Avenue. Opposite center: *Alicia Markova and Hugh Laing in the title roles of Antony Tudor's* Romeo and Juliet. *Laing was one of the chief exponents of Tudor's choreography and appeared in nearly all of his works until the early '50s.* Opposite bottom: *Markova with Anton Dolin in* Giselle, *the ballet most closely associated with their partnership in the '30s and '40s.* Left: *Mikhail Baryshnikov in Tudor's* Shadowplay.

He showed his fleetness of foot in Ashton's Neapolitan divertissement in Act III of *Swan Lake;* he was the buoyant Jester in Ashton's *Cinderella.* Perhaps his most memorable characterizations were Bottom in *The Dream,* the lovable bumpkin who is temporarily turned into an ass as part of Oberon's plot to win his point with Titania, and the endearingly silly Alain of the red umbrella in Ashton's version of *La Fille Mal Gardée.* In his farewell season with the Royal, prior to taking on his new responsibilities as Director of the National Ballet of Canada in 1976, Grant created his final Ashton role, that of the tolerant, doting husband and father, Yslaev, in the ballet adaptation of Turgenev's *A Month in the Country.* It seems unlikely that anyone who takes on this role in the future will quite match the inspired self-absorption and bluff tenderness that Grant brought to it. Grant helped to establish and has left behind a rich repertoire for the character dancer. For example, Wayne Sleep, a short, boyish-looking virtuoso who portrayed Grant's kite-flying son in *A Month in the Country,* has Grant to thank in a sense for several of the roles he now performs with such high-flying flair.

Because Grant was from the Commonwealth, he was snapped up by the Sadler's Wells company the moment his talents were recognized and was thrust into major roles. But according to Margot Fonteyn's recent autobiography, Ninette de Valois steadfastly refused to bolster her diminished ranks of male dancers after the war with danseurs from abroad. Young men such as Michael Somes lost some of the most vital performing years a male dancer has, from age twenty-three to twenty-seven; Somes came home from the war seriously injured as well. But de Valois accepted the setback to their careers and took the long view. "I will not do it," Fonteyn quotes her as saying. "If I take any of these foreign boys it will discourage our own dancers and we will never develop a tradition for male dancers in England. It is not fair to our boys." She was not altogether without male resources, however. Somes made the long struggle to regain his technique and became Fonteyn's regular partner during the late forties and fifties, creating roles with her in such Ashton ballets as *Daphnis and Chloe, Cinderella,* and the delicate, full-length fantasy ballet *Ondine,* as well as performing with her in the classics. Soon de Valois was adding others to the ranks, danseurs such as Brian Shaw, David Blair, and Donald MacLeary. But it was not until the advent of the Bolshoi Ballet in 1956 and the arrival in the West of Rudolf Nureyev, soon to be resident with the Royal Ballet, that British male dancing was galvanized to attain the heights it has now achieved. By giving Nureyev a foothold in her company—however tenuous and impermanent—de Valois did more for the technical standards of her danseurs than perhaps even her farsightedness could anticipate.

Opposite top: *Robert Helpmann, one of ballet's great masters of the art of makeup, prepares to perform the character role of the evil fairy Carabosse in* Sleeping Beauty. *Opposite bottom: Michael Somes and Margot Fonteyn, the great partnership of British ballet in the 1950s, in Ashton's* Daphnis and Chloe, *a ballet created for these special dancers. Above left: British character dancer Alexander Grant in one of his most famous roles, the suitor Alain in Ashton's* La Fille Mal Gardée. *Above: Helpmann in the title role of Dame Ninette de Valois's* The Rake's Progress, *based on Hogarth's paintings, in which Helpmann brilliantly portrayed the Rake's descent into madness. Left: Sir Frederick Ashton as one of the Ugly Sisters in his own version of* Cinderella; *drawing on the British pantomime tradition, the role is danced* en travesti.

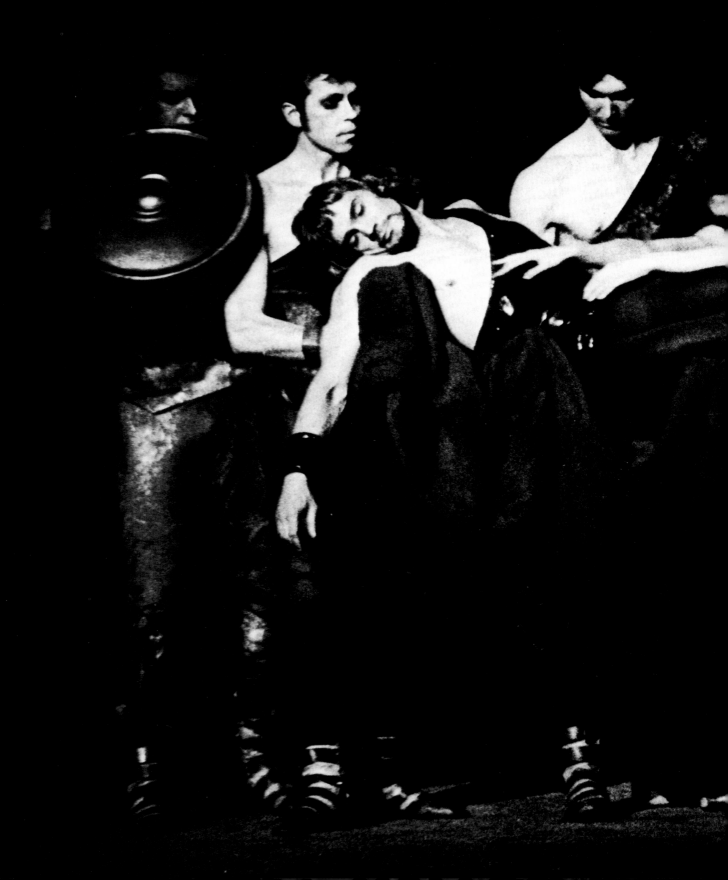

5

Swan Song to Spartacus: The Danseur and Soviet Ballet

The Russians have led the way in reestablishing the danseur to a position of equality with the ballerina. When most people in the West think of Russian dance today, its unreserved athleticism comes to mind first: magnificent leaps, breath-taking supports, spirited and often stunning technical feats that seem to mock the laws of gravity and the physical limitations of the human body—in short, things that have become largely the province of Russian male dancing.

Although the Soviet Union may have the best-trained dancers in the world—the products of state-supported schools and teachers who are artistic descendants of those who produced Pavlova and Nijinsky—their dancers by our eclectic standards appear to be given the least variety of choreography to dance. The isolation from the mainstream of Western innovation that generally characterizes Soviet ballet permits few outsiders to study in its schools, dance with its companies, or choreograph for its dancers. This isolation has been a primary factor in the defection of some of Russia's greatest talent. There has been little new blood infused into Russian ballet in the twentieth century; and what innovations do occur seem scarcely experimental by our criteria and often meet with a lukewarm reception in the West.

Russian dancers today are heirs to a long and honored tradition, which has proved to be amazingly resilient in the face of artistic upheavals and political challenges. With the overthrow of Czar Nicholas II in 1917, Russian art was thrust into an entirely new setting. In ballet, the Revolution produced a dramatic swing away from the Petipa influence, with its stilted, aristocratic settings and its emphasis on the glittering ballerina. Beginning in the 1920s, Russian ballets focused on propagandistic stories, with heavy emphasis on sports and athleticism in dance. By the 1960s, Yuri Grigorovich, artistic director and chief choreographer of the Bolshoi Ballet, had created a repertoire containing strong leading roles for male dancers; he also insisted on less mime and more pure dancing, returning to the more sumptuous, musical productions popular before the Revolution. But largely because of international politics, little was known in the West about Soviet art until the decade following 1956, when the Bolshoi made its first impressive appearance in London.

Since the Revolution, the Russians who have decided to make their homes in the West have formed a hard core of classical dancers regarded as leading exponents of ballet. Pierre Vladimirov, for example, a great danseur noble of pre-Revolutionary times, made his home in New York City, where he taught generations of Americans the Russian style of dancing that had flourished under the czars. Anna Pavlova, Russian-born and Maryinsky-trained, made her home in England after the Revolution and toured the world proselytizing for the cause of ballet.

One of Pavlova's most famous partners after she settled in the West was the Russian Mikhail Mordkin, a danseur who finally opted for a career in New York, where he founded a school and company, predecessor to American Ballet Theatre. Another distinguished Russian dancer who settled in New York was Michel Fokine, who, for all the genius of his earlier years, seemed to lose much of his creative impetus once he was no longer associated with Diaghilev's Ballets Russes. Nijinsky, of course, is the most famous Russian danseur to leave Russia. He never returned after the Revolution; nor did the impresario Diaghilev. Oddly enough, it was Diaghilev's company—with its distinctly avant-garde tendencies and a style that had little to do with native Russian ballet—that formed the West's early (and often inaccurate) image of the best of "Russian" dance. The successors to Diaghilev's company, after his death in 1929, were several organizations that called themselves Ballets Russes; they toured Europe and America until the early 1960s, thus helping to perpetuate the popular misconception of Russian ballet. Just about *any* ballet, it seemed, had to be Russian. By the time the last of these troupes folded, there had been a

Preceding pages: *Death of a hero in Soviet ballet: Vladimir Vasiliev of the Bolshoi in the title role of* Spartacus. *Above: Natalia Bessmertnova as the Swan Queen Odette and Mikhail Lavrovsky as Siegfried in the Bolshoi's* Swan Lake.

Opposite: *Vladimir Vasiliev.*
Left: *Vyacheslav Gordeyev and his
wife, Nadezhda Pavlova, in the*
Nutcracker *Pas de Deux.* Below:
Maris Liepa in the Bolshoi's
Anna Karenina. Bottom:
*Alexander Godunov with Maya
Plisetskaya in Roland Petit's*
La Rose Malade.

sensational awakening, produced by the arrival of the Bolshoi Ballet, in London in 1956 and in New York in 1959. Much of our prior knowledge of contemporary Russian ballet had been gleaned from old films, from occasional reports or articles originating within the Soviet Union, from infrequent tours of Soviet stars, or from rarer firsthand accounts by Western travelers who ventured behind the Iron Curtain. Our knowledge was so limited that we were unprepared for the real thing.

Given the upheavals of the Russian Revolution, it might seem unusual that an institution that had been the private plaything of the ruling class would be allowed to survive, but such was the case with ballet in Russia. Anatol Lunasharsky, the first Soviet Commissar of Education, was himself an enlightened and cultured man who felt that the ballet was worth preserving. However, ballet's connections with the czar's court brought it under close scrutiny and frequent criticism. Fortunately, dance was recognized as an art that the Russians did uniquely well, and the decision to allow ballet to continue and to provide government support for its schools and companies resulted in the creation of some of the finest dancers of our century—a handful of whom, by defection, served the West as prime examples of what a system that reveres its dancers can produce.

The first generation of Soviet dancers (which included choreographer George Balanchine) was very much under the shadow of the czarist regime. Prior to the Revolution, dancing had become intellectually arid, in spite of the efforts of crusaders such as Fokine and Gorsky to infuse it with some fresh perspectives. Petipa has been blamed for this. Indeed, his leading male dancer was Pavel Gerdt, premier danseur at the Maryinsky from 1866 until 1916—a man with impeccable style but whose limitations (including only a modest technique) affected Petipa's choreography for male dancers for many years. Gerdt was secure at the Maryinsky because of his contract, which guaranteed leading roles; the effect of his presence was felt on dance as a whole—and by male dancers in particular—for a long time.

For a short time, the Revolution brought revolutionary artistic freedom to Russia, and the effect on male dancing was enormous. To the classics were added new works with innovative movement that seemed quite avant-garde for the period: barefoot dancing (an innovation that the authorities had vetoed when Fokine tried to introduce it at the Maryinsky), social dancing, "erotic" dancing, and national folk dances, which have a particularly rich heritage in Russia and which, it was believed, would help to unite the diverse political and ethnic elements that made up the new Soviet Union. Much of this folk work relied on expansive, demanding techniques traditionally developed in male dancers.

Scenes from Ivan the Terrible, *choreographed for the Bolshoi Ballet by Yuri Grigorovich.* Opposite: *Vladimir Vasiliev in the title role, with Natalia Bessmertnova as his wife.* Above: *Vasiliev as the demented Ivan.*

During the 1920s an inspired teacher, Agrippina Vaganova, undertook the codification of the Russian system. Vaganova standardized Soviet dance teaching, reducing the differences between the Kirov and Bolshoi schools, and her syllabus became the basis for the Soviet method. Her system strongly adhered to a classical base, which would result in the finest-trained classical dancers in the world, but which also made experiments in "modern" choreography difficult to realize. "If art, indeed, should reflect contemporary life, it does not mean that classical examples of its past should disappear," she wrote. Separate classes were taught for boys and girls—an arrangement that unfortunately is not economically feasible for most schools in the West, although special classes for boys, particularly, help to build their confidence at a time when they are maturing more slowly than girls, as well as emphasizing the differences in their technical vocabulary.

Two of the leading exponents of the new directions in which Soviet dance began to move during the 1920s were Fyodor Lopokov and Kasyan Goleizovsky. The careers of both men were long and influential, and in the 1920s they laid the foundation for what later. became the characteristic style of Soviet ballet: a concern for polemics and an overriding emphasis on virtuosity, athleticism, and stage heroics.

Lopokov was a leading classicist and came to be one of the great experts on Russia's classical heritage. In this respect, he is a direct descendant of Petipa. He was the first to use the original 1877 score for *Swan Lake,* as well as the first to give that ballet's evil magician, von Rothbart, a dancing role, rather than the usual mime. Lopokov worked on the creation of ballets that used movement from sports events, nightclubs, and everyday life. He introduced acrobatics into ballet during the 1920s. And one of the most spectacular facets of Soviet choreography —the lift in which the danseur supports the ballerina high above his head on one hand, as seen today in ballets from *Spring Waters* to *Spartacus*—was first introduced in Lopokov's ballet *Ice Maiden* (1927). His *Taras Bulba,* adapted from a story by Nikolai Gogol and later rechoreographed by Boris Fenster (whose version we have seen in the West), was a highly charged Cossack competition, a ballet designed primarily for men in colorful costumes performing a wide range of extremely difficult steps that demanded agility, audacity, and strength.

Cyril Beaumont, the English writer and critic, has described

Left: *The Moiseyev Dance Company's tours outside the Soviet Union have helped to familiarize the world with the spectacular athletic feats of Russian folk dance. Here, Alexander Strelkov is seen leaping in* Gopak, *a traditional dance of the Ukraine.* Below: *Sergei Vikulov and Gabriella Komleva performing in the Leningrad Kirov Ballet production of* La Bayadère.

a Soviet ballet called *The Golden Age* (1931), which, although no longer performed, gives us some idea of the new works produced in the Soviet Union during this period. Since there was a shortage of plots for new ballets with the necessary political elements, a contest was held in 1929, and *The Golden Age* was the winner. Choreographically speaking, the ballet was a collective effort, the work of four choreographers, including Vasily Vainonen (whose most famous work outside the Soviet Union would be his 1932 ballet *Flames of Paris*).

Set in a "large capitalist city" at an industrial exhibition, *The Golden Age* depicts, in a cartoonlike series of episodes, the conflicts between Fascists (and their cohorts, the capitalists) and Soviet citizens (and defenders of the downtrodden). The Fascists are depicted as decadent and cowardly, in need of the support of a well-armed, brutal battalion of police, while the Soviets are wholesome, freedom-loving heroes. While the Fascists are wheeled around in splendidly upholstered chairs, the champions of the exploited are portrayed by a football team, a black boxer (who is beaten unfairly in a boxing match with a white Fascist), and Women of the Communist Soviet Youth. There are dances for football players, a pas de trois for three male athletes, a fight-and-escape scene, and divertissements based on discus throwing, tennis, fencing, basketball, and javelin throwing. At the ballet's conclusion, there is a tap dance (advertising a capitalist product called Superfine Boot Polish), a polka, an orgiastic cancan, a "Dance of Reconciliation of all Classes," and so on.

Heavy-handed as it may seem, this simplistic moralizing found great favor in the Soviet Union in the 1920s and was soon widely accepted in the ballet. One is able to link the antifascist sentiments of *The Golden Age* with more recent Soviet works such as *Spartacus,* in which the Roman troops (the oppressors of the slaves) go so far as to do a choreographed goose step, more than a little reminiscent of the Nazis.

During the 1920s, the Soviet Union was too busy recovering from war and famine to take more than cursory notice of its artists—dancers and choreographers included—although acceptance of government support implied that the works created be true to proletarian ideals. (Anything too progressive, such as dancing for the sake of pure dancing, was regarded as a bourgeois distortion.) In April of 1932, however, the Communist Party issued an official Resolution called "On the Reconstruction of Literary and Artistic Organizations," which spelled the end of the easy-going freedom that had been possible during the previous decade. Fortunately for the greatly enhanced art of male dancing, the changes that had taken place had become very much a part of the system that had Party approval. One of the official criteria for all art was that it contain a positive political statement, usually in conjunction with a serious theme.

Called socialist realism, the guidelines also instructed that the arts be accessible to great masses of people—that they be easy to understand. It was important that at least one character represent heroic ideals and that the audience be able to identify with him—and this character tended to be male. Works such as *The Red Poppy, Flames of Paris, Legend of Love,* and *Laurencia* represented themes that found approval under socialist realism. Even the classics had to be reexamined: *Swan Lake* was given a happy ending, to show the conquest of Good (Odette and Siegfried) over Evil (von Rothbart and Odile), the penultimate scene being a skirmish of gymnastic proportions between the two men. A Jester was introduced into the first act (still retained in Soviet productions) and his demanding dancing role also served to comment on the real status of socially divided kings and fools. In *Giselle,* the Soviet interpreters saw the tragedy as the natural consequence of an aristocracy (in the person of Albrecht) that dominated simpler peasants (represented by Giselle). And as the dominant character in the drama, Albrecht was given more dancing to perform.

The first so-called revolutionary ballet to hold the stage was *The Red Poppy,* choreographed in 1927 by Vasily Tikhomirov and Lev Lashchilin. The story's protagonist is a female Chinese dancer named Tao Hoa, who falls in love with a Soviet sea captain and dies during an uprising against European imperialists in pre-Revolutionary China. The ballet contained a number of very popular ensembles and divertissements for sailors of various nationalities, and the strength of the choreography, as Cyril Beaumont relates, lay in the number of dances for men; its weakness was a lack of any outstanding dances for women!

During this same period—the 1930s—danseur Vakhtang Chabukiani came to prominence, and his greatest roles, considered important in the development during this period of the so-called heroic style of Soviet male dancing, are connected with landmarks in Soviet ballet. As Jerome in Vasily Vainonen's *Flames of Paris* (1932), a ballet dealing with the French Revolution in highly sympathetic, "dictatorship of the proletariat" terms, Chabukiani was able to use his unique talents as an actor-dancer to their fullest range and power; his performance was later filmed and shown in the West in the early 1950s. He is said to have represented the Soviet ideal as a dancer because of his athletic physique, his forceful personality, and the dynamics of his technique—qualities still valid in the Soviet Union and attributed to contemporary Soviet male dancers such as Vladimir Vasiliev, Yuri Vladimirov, and Mikhail Lavrovsky.

Two other successes with which Chabukiani is associated are Zakharov's *The Fountain of Bakhchiserai* (1934), based on Pushkin, and Lavrovsky's *The Prisoner of the Caucasus* (1937), also from Pushkin. Chabukiani's own three-act ballet *Laurencia* (after Lope de Vega's *Fuente Ovejuna*) was first performed at

Top: *Dancers of the Bolshoi Ballet in class.* Left: *Mikhail Lavrovsky and Natalia Bessmertnova in Yuri Grigorovich's* Legend of Love. Above: *Vakhtang Chabukiani in* Flames of Paris, *a ballet set in France during the French Revolution. It was included in the film* Stars of the Russian Ballet, *which was released in the United States in the mid-1950s and helped to whet the Western appetite for more Russian dancing.*

109

Top: *Moiseyev dancers in* Partisans. Above: *Valery Panov in costume for* Le Corsaire, *at Caesarea in Israel.* Right:
Yuri Soloviev as Danila the Stone Cutter in The Stone Flower.

the Kirov in 1939, with Chabukiani himself and ballerina Natalia Dudinskaya in the leading roles. (Twenty-five years later, Nureyev staged the pas de six from *Laurencia* for the Royal Ballet, having learned it as a student; he was in fact much influenced by Chabukiani's frequent augmentation of the danseur's role in the classics.) Chabukiani's duet *Etude* is familiar to Western audiences, having been performed here as part of the divertissement programs that the Soviets favor on their tours. It too exploits the virile technique, making use of complicated lifts and the dramatic waving of draperies.

Leonid Lavrovsky was the first choreographer of the "modern" classic *Romeo and Juliet*. His version was premiered in 1940 with the title roles danced by the great ballerina Galina Ulanova and Konstantin Sergeyev, a danseur noble whose career as dancer, choreographer, and administrator was linked with the fortunes of the Kirov. One of many works choreographed to a literary theme in Russian ballet, Lavrovsky's *Romeo,* a landmark in dance history, used classical dance to enhance characterization, giving psychological motivation to movement. Influenced by the theatrical work in Leningrad in the 1920s, Lavrovsky believed that as much attention should be given to making a role believable as to the actual dancing. Thus, his choreography heightened realism and focused on the inherent social message in each of his dramatic situations. "Ballet is a choreographic play," he said, "in which dancing must arise naturally from mimed action, or the mimed action from the logical sequence of the dancing."

Romeo and Juliet has been rechoreographed a number of times in the West, by choreographers such as Frederick Ashton, Kenneth MacMillan, and John Cranko, among others; its lushly orchestrated score by Prokofiev is keenly sensitive to the musical demands of the dancing and makes the ballet one of the mainstays of any company that includes it in its repertoire. It was televised around the world in its entirety in celebration of the Bolshoi's two-hundredth anniversary; appropriately, Lavrovsky's son, Mikhail, now a leading dancer with the Bolshoi, was given the honor of performing the title role for this special occasion.

After the Second World War, socialist realism began to fall from favor, and its proponents found themselves in eclipse by the late 1950s. In an account on the state of Soviet art after the war, Brooks Atkinson wrote that the arts were "reactionary and moribund. . . . There is little opportunity, individual enterprise and experiment. . . . Soviet art contains just as much hokum and bathos as ours, without adding occasional works of originality that compensate for failure."

The policies of isolationism had taken their toll on artistic development, and by the early 1950s the arts had begun to shift away from hard-line party attitudes toward creative output. In dance, polemics began to be replaced by a concern for the dancing itself. The shift received added impetus from George Balanchine's visit to the Soviet Union (after an absence of thirty-eight years) with his New York City Ballet in 1962, when he displayed his neoclassical style of dance: nineteenth-century technique refreshed by innovation and experiment. It was also a result of the influence of the classicist Lopokov on Russia's rising young choreographer, Yuri Grigorovich.

Igor Moiseyev had sounded the challenge in 1952 when he wrote that "all our latest productions suffer from a common fault, the poverty of dance form; the striving after content and the depiction of it are taken as a denial of the leading role of [the] dance [itself]." At first, the exponents of the old Soviet art forms were not affected by the changes taking place, but the challenges from younger men, including Igor Moiseyev (who established what is now the foremost folk ensemble in the world) and Grigorovich, eventually won strong support from other young Soviet choreographers and dancers.

As director of the Bolshoi Ballet, Grigorovich has turned out to be the Soviet Union's most important choreographer since Fokine. Employing a style that is strong and straightforward, he has exerted influence in two important areas: the male dancer has been given a wealth of new, challenging material and, subsequently, greater emphasis in performance; and classical dance for the sake of dancing has found its way back into Soviet ballet. Today, heavy-handed polemics tend to be avoided. Grigorovich's *Legend of Love* (1961) for the Kirov had dances of symphonic nature; his epic *Spartacus* (1968), a reworking of a theme that had been tried unsuccessfully in the past, was the most successful ballet in the Soviet Union since Lavrovsky's *Romeo and Juliet;* his *Ivan the Terrible* (1975), based on Prokofiev's score, shared a similar success. Grigorovich has excelled in the classics as well, lending new life to a familiar work with his restaging of *Nutcracker,* for example. In his years at the Bolshoi he has built up a young company of dancers who share his enthusiasm for ballet and has given the company a very different look from what was first seen in the West two decades ago.

When Moscow's Bolshoi Ballet made its historic debut in London in 1956, a large Western audience saw for the first time since the Revolution what was being produced by the rigorous Russian system of training dancers. The Bolshoi dancers were living proof of what could be attained on the ballet stage with proper training and perseverance. The company's full-length ballets—*Romeo and Juliet, Swan Lake, The Stone Flower*— projected an epic scale and sheer vastness unknown to the West; the short selections, such as an excerpt from *The Foun-*

tain of Bakhchiserai, showed off a virtuosic technique that had seemed impossible to achieve. Never had we seen such lifts and leaps, such athleticism and flamboyance, particularly for the male dancers. At the Bolshoi's Western premiere Yuri Zhdanov danced with prima ballerina assoluta Galina Ulanova in Leonid Lavrovsky's production of the Soviet classic *Romeo and Juliet.* The Bolshoi *Swan Lake* included Nicolai Fadeyechev, whose excellent acting, technique, and partnering made him a danseur especially suited to the Romantic style, and Georgi Farmaniantz, one of Russia's finest character dancers, with unusual range and virtuosity. A revelation was the performance given by Gleb Yevdokimov, a *demi-caractère* dancer, who led the Tatar dances in an excerpt from *The Fountain of Bakhchiserai,* a ballet firmly rooted in the tradition of socialist realism. In 1959, the Bolshoi's trip to the United States established equally vivid impressions: Vladimir Vasiliev, who was seen to much acclaim as Danila the stonecutter in Grigorovich's *The Stone Flower,* and who is considered today to be one of the greatest dancers in the world; Vladimir Levashev, a famous character dancer; as well as Fadeyechev, Yevdokimov, and Zhdanov.

Russian danseurs such as Nicolai Fadeyechev were found to be superb partners, although the role of the danseur noble seemed to have been neglected somewhat in favor of a more athletic personality, which was more in line with the Soviet concern for heroics. In the Bolshoi company as a whole, Westerners discovered that greater importance had been given to character roles than was the case in the West. The Soviets were strongly theatrical—many considered them to be overly explicit —and the acting was given equal weight with the dancing.

The Bolshoi's dancing was also compared, unflatteringly, with the works of acrobats. Such comments were heard most frequently in discussions of the shorter divertissements, concert pieces, and "highlights" designed to showcase pyrotechnics, in such works as *Spring Waters* (a daring duet), the Sabre Dance from *Gayané, Gopak,* the pas de trois from *The Ocean and the Pearls,* the pas de deux from *Nutcracker,* and the polonaise and krakoviak from *Ivan Susanin.*

Westerners were unused to such emphasis on spectacle and the spectacular, and found that the evening-length works had serious dramatic flaws. The broad style of acting—about as subtle·as semaphores—with its emphasis on melodramatic moments, was regarded by some as having overstepped the bounds of good taste. The best of what the Bolshoi brought to the West, however, made such an indelibly strong impression that it was soon being copied—although not too successfully at first, since the Russian technique requires special training, including lifting weights.

In 1961, the aristocratic Kirov Ballet (known as the Maryinsky before the Revolution) made its debut in the West.

Again, Western audiences were deeply impressed, this time by the dancers' musicality and lyricism. Dramatics were not the forte of the Kirov, not to the same degree they had been the Bolshoi's, and its dancing of the classics struck many as being "purer," more controlled and sustained. Again, we were introduced to a host of dancers whose performances far exceeded anything we had seen. These included such notables as Yuri Korneyev, Sergei Vikulov (who partnered Natalia Makarova), Rudolf Nureyev, and Yuri Soloviev, who was destined to become one of the West's favorite Russian dancers.

Soloviev, born in Leningrad in 1940 and trained at the Leningrad Choreographic Institute, was—like Nureyev, Valery Panov, and Baryshnikov—a student of the renowned teacher Alexander Pushkin. He joined the Kirov in 1958 and was quickly performing leading roles, in spite of a physique that to our eyes made him seem less than ideally suited to the classics. He was not really handsome, and with his heavy thighs, he was not elegant in repose. But he wasn't earthbound: he was a dancer who, propelled by those thighs, could seem to hover in

the air, and the sweetness and joy he projected to his audience made him loved.

When Nureyev defected at the end of the Kirov's 1961 performances in Paris, Soloviev quickly became the undisputed male star of the company for Western audiences. (Valery Panov, who was transferred from Leningrad's Maly company to the Kirov after Nureyev's defection to fill some of his roles, performed a somewhat different, character repertoire—and before he was allowed to emigrate from Russia in 1974, he made only one appearance in the West.) Of Soloviev's appearances in some of Nureyev's roles in London, where the Kirov next performed, without Nureyev, one critic wrote: "Yuri Soloviev, who consists of a mop of blond hair and a mass of steel muscles, can jump and spin breathtakingly and be utterly engaging the while." Soloviev took the London ballet audience by storm. At one performance, his Bluebird (excerpted from *Sleeping Beauty* to display his virtuosity) had to be repeated to satisfy the audience's enthusiasm; on another occasion his fans followed him from the stage door of the theater to his hotel, applauding all the way.

Soloviev appeared not only in the classics, but in modern Russian works as well, such as *The Stone Flower* and *Leningrad Symphony,* and his phenomenal elevation and ballon were so admired that they were compared with Nijinsky's. Of his performance in *The Stone Flower,* Clive Barnes of the *New York Times* wrote: "He whirled around the stage in a step then virtually new to the West, a double assemblé. In effect, it looked impossible, but it also looked wonderful." Sad to say, Yuri Soloviev died early in 1977 at the height of his career, an apparent suicide. His art is preserved for us on film, in the Kirov's *Sleeping Beauty,* for example, and perhaps this is what he wanted: to be remembered at the apex of the leap, at the height of his powers as a dancer, before age robbed him of his technique. Or perhaps, like his former comrades Nureyev, Panov, Makarova, and Baryshnikov, he was feeling stifled as an artist by the Soviet system. We may never know. He was a bright comet that flashed across the Russian stage, and perhaps his death marks the end of an era in Russian dance. Without Soloviev and the stars who have cast their lot with ballet in the West, the Kirov ranks are thinned of major dancers; the company has scarcely been seen in Western dance capitals for several years. It is inevitably losing some of its long preeminence in the world of ballet.

The influence that both the Bolshoi and the Kirov had on Western ballet was reciprocal: soon American and European companies—both ballet and modern dance—were traveling to Russia, and the Russians were borrowing and stealing from the West almost as shamelessly as the West had borrowed and stolen from the Russians. For example, after the famous Bolshoi

Opposite: *Nina Sorokina and Mikhail Lavrovsky of the Bolshoi in the Diana and Acteon Pas de Deux from* Esmeralda. *Above:* Valery Panov leads dancers of the Kirov Ballet in Oleg Vinogradov's spirited Gorianka.

choreographer Leonid Lavrovsky visited the United States with the Bolshoi in 1959 and saw the New York musical *West Side Story* on Broadway, he returned to Russia and choreographed a modern, American-style ballet, *Night City,* about a gang of street toughs. "One fist fight between the hero and the gang," UPI reported, "is reminiscent of the gang fight in *West Side Story,* and in *Night City* the hero also dies, stabbed by the gang." The works of other American choreographers, such as Ailey, Arpino, Graham, Taylor, and our adopted Balanchine, made an even more marked impression on the Soviets.

Travel to the Soviet Union is now commonplace; this and international competitions at Moscow, Varna (in Bulgaria), and elsewhere help provide us with more firsthand information on what's happening in Soviet ballet today. (Nureyev and Baryshnikov were first known to the West through films made at such competitions.) However, it is still relatively difficult to acquire current information on a regular basis. During a recent compilation of material for a dictionary of ballet, 200 questionnaires were mailed to authorities on ballet within the Soviet Union. There was not a single reply, although other "unofficial" sources within the Soviet Union finally provided the much-needed material. Fear and secrecy continue to hamper the flow of communications.

Who are the talented young dancers? Westerners are allowed to see only a few. If an important danseur like Valery Panov is allowed to make only one performance at New York City's Madison Square Garden, as he did in 1960 with the Kirov, and then is summoned back to Russia, who else may there be that the authorities do not allow to come even that far? In Soviet ballet, there is neither room nor flexibility for a colorful or rebellious individual such as Panov or Nureyev. Nureyev's defection was, in its time, a celebrated news event; Panov's, however, became a cause célèbre, especially in light of the cruelty of Soviet officials in not allowing him to dance, or even to rehearse or take class, during the two years that the question of his emigration was pending. Unlike Nureyev, Panov and his wife, Galina Ragozina, had applied for a visa to leave Russia and travel to Israel, where they hoped to settle. They were all but confined to their apartment, lost their well-earned status as leading dancers with the Kirov, and found themselves engulfed in a sea of red tape. After two years, the couple was finally allowed to leave the Soviet Union—mainly because of the pressure brought on the Soviets by Panov supporters around the world. But Valery Panov was at an age (his mid-thirties) when it was nearly impossible for him to regain the strength and virtuosity that had been his prior to confinement. The Panovs now dance as guests with ballet companies in Europe and America.

Of those dancers who remain behind as honored members

of Soviet society, Yuri Vladimirov is one of the Bolshoi's most energetic and forceful performers. The Bolshoi's Vladimir Vasiliev is of the same generation that produced Nureyev and Soloviev and is an artist with an international following that rivals the accolades given to superstars in the West. By means of a dynamic virtuosity, he has made an important contribution to the renaissance of strong male dancing in Soviet ballet. Mikhail Baryshnikov in his recent book *Baryshnikov at Work* has credited Vasiliev, with "his tauter, much more stretched-out line and impact," as having displayed "a male partnering style that could be considered revolutionary." Vasiliev has performed in such Soviet classics as *The Little Humpbacked Horse* and *The Stone Flower;* the leading roles in *Spartacus* and *Ivan the Terrible* were created with him in mind. When *Spartacus* was first performed in the United States in 1975, Vasiliev's elevation and agility in the title role were the subject of much praise; he was described by the American press as the personification of "power and virility"; and a British critic wrote that he "accomplished the seemingly impossible with such consummate ease . . . that he is able to avoid appearing acrobatic, as so many Soviet male dancers do." With his wife, ballerina Yekaterina Maximova, Vasiliev occasionally appears as a guest performer outside the Soviet Union—an unusual honor.

Vasiliev is often compared and contrasted with Maris Liepa, another danseur with the Bolshoi who has won the admiration of an international audience. Like Vasiliev, Liepa has

Scenes from Grigorovich's Spartacus, *one of the most popular works by a contemporary choreographer in the Bolshoi's repertoire; it features especially strong choreography for male dancers. Opposite: Maris Liepa as Crassus, the Roman general who crushes the slaves' revolt. Top left: Mikhail Lavrovsky as the slave leader Spartacus. Top right: Vladimir Vasiliev in the same role. Left: Vasiliev as Spartacus with Yekaterina Maximova as Phrygia, his wife. Above: Liepa with Svetlana Adikhrieva as Aegina.*

made an especially strong impression in virtuosic ballets that demand strong acting, such as *Spartacus* and *Ivan the Terrible*. In London, he was called "the Laurence Olivier of the dance," a response to the strong, individualistic style of acting that he combines with his versatile talents as a dancer. Liepa's range of performance includes films and television, as well as the avant-garde. His popularity in Moscow is so great that he was allowed to put on a solo program—a very rare honor. His performances drew full houses—not unlike the programs staged in the West by Nureyev and several of his "friends."

Although Russian danseurs such as Vasiliev and Liepa have achieved the status of international stars, there is a tendency in the Soviet Union to emphasize the ballets first, the choreographers second, and the individual dancers last. The less known about the dancers—the less focus on any singularly accomplished artist—the less chance there is for embarrassment in the future. Relative anonymity for the dancers acts in the Soviet's favor in that it makes the West a less secure and less attractive place to be, especially if the West has heard little or nothing about young talent.

There is also a tendency to keep dancing and dancers in the family. There is a good reason for this—a dancer with strong ties to the homeland is less likely to rock the bureaucratic boat. Also, Soviet dancers tend to marry other Soviet dancers rather than finding spouses outside their profession. Hence we find descendants of Petipa, Gerdt, Legat, Lavrovsky, Gorsky, Zakharov, and Sergeyev, to name only a few, still among the higher echelons of performers. In the Bolshoi, there is pairing off at the top, as well: Mikhail Lavrovsky is married to Ludmila Semenyaka, Vasiliev to Yekaterina Maximova, Grigorovich to Natalia Bessmertnova, Vladimirov to Nina Sorokina, Gordeyev to Nadezhda Pavlova. A glance at the Kirov's roster reveals equally impressive matches. Valery Panov and Galina Ragozina were Kirov dancers of renown; and Konstantin Sergeyev and Natalia Dudinskaya have left a lasting, if controversial, impression on the Kirov as dancers, administrators, and teachers.

Other questions come to mind regarding Soviet ballet. What, for example, do the epic-length works regularly produced by the large companies look like? Only two have been shown in the West in their entirety: Grigorovich's *Spartacus* and *Ivan the Terrible*. The West knows only the two major ballet companies—one from Leningrad (the Kirov) and one from Moscow (the Bolshoi)—and a handful of regional Russian folk companies. But what kind of work is being produced by the dozens of other companies reputed to have strong professional standards and status within the state-supported system? Although Soviet officials are willing to answer some of these questions, there is still a protective cloud obscuring much of the current activity.

We do know that Russian dancers are usually given a twenty-year contract with an individual company, with the promise of renewal or retirement with pension when the contract runs out. Many of the retired dancers become teachers, assuming positions with any number of academies and companies across the Soviet Union. In the past decade there has been an increasing exchange of technique and talent between ballet and sports, such as skating and gymnastics. In recent Olympic competitions, young Russian athletes have achieved international recognition in their fields partly because of their training in ballet. Ice skaters working with top Soviet choreographers have begun to establish a balletic style that requires years of ballet training. Likewise, ballet dancers have found that the introduction of gymnastics has helped to improve their musicality, pace, and ease of performance. Having once put sports into their ballets, the Soviets are now putting ballet into their sports.

Dancing in Russia today is big business, with over thirty full-time state-supported schools and companies, and in order for the art to remain vigorous and expressive it must of necessity continue to grow and change. The thought of creating plotless ballets, for example, is no longer inconceivable; American and European visitors have changed that perspective. There is even some "modern" work taking place, in the American and German vein, although most Russian dancers by training and temperament are not yet prepared for such a major shift away from the classical base. But the cultural cross-pollination has had an inestimable effect on all of us. We have seen what they can do, and we want to do it. They have watched us—and some of them have wanted to dance our way so much that they have left Russia for good in order to do so.

We have seen the high regard accorded Soviet dancers—the guaranteed incomes, the comfortable apartments, the educational opportunities, the pensions. But there are still reasons in the Soviet Union—artistic reasons—for discontent. One of the most famous among the discontented is Rudolf Nureyev, a man who helped bring some of the best of the Russian system to the West—and with it established a new image, based on the Soviet model, for male dancers around the world.

Rehearsals of Konstantin Sergeyev's Hamlet at the Rossi Street Studio in Leningrad. Left: Mikhail Baryshnikov in the title role. Top and above: Valery Panov also as Hamlet, before he left the Soviet Union. Panov was originally slated to perform the role, but when he requested permission to emigrate to Israel, he was barred from any further rehearsals or performances.

Rudolf Nureyev, Artist and Superstar

On the day of his fabled defection at Le Bourget Airport outside Paris in 1961, Nureyev brought no luggage with him—only some intangibles: his great talent, a highly polished technique, and the knowledge of the Russian classics, which he had absorbed during his training and few seasons with the Kirov Ballet as one of that company's leading young danseurs. Since then, with ingenuity, persistence, and native wit, he has made good on his ambitions to dance everything, always and everywhere. He has said that it seems only fitting that a dancer who "lives" on stage as he does should have the right to die on stage as well. A dramatic metaphor—but one that seems curiously appropriate as a possible future close to his turbulent career.

He had danced the classics at home; they were in his blood, a part of that same Maryinsky training that had been Nijinsky's. Like Nijinsky, he too had been something of a prodigy; he performed roles like Albrecht and Siegfried within two years after graduating from the Leningrad Kirov school, and was invited by the Kirov's leading ballerina, Natalia Dudinskaya, to partner her in his first performance as a full-fledged member of the Leningrad company. Nearly everything he learned in those years has been put to use, and often improved upon—from Vakhtang Chabukiani's bravura choreography for male roles in ballets such as *Le Corsaire,* to the art of partnering a number of different ballerinas. A late starter in his formal ballet training, he has capitalized since his days as a student on his ability to absorb a role quickly, to learn steps for a solo in the course of a single rehearsal, as well as on his virtuosity and strong sense of dramatic moment. From early in his performing career he was never satisfied just to copy other dancers, no matter how distinguished they might be. He insisted on bringing his own interpretation to each of the roles he learned—which now number nearly eight dozen. "Don't think the public wants to see one good dancer after another, all exactly alike," he says, "It is only when some individual quality is there that it becomes interesting." When no contemporary choreographer was creating a new role for him to dance, he would simply reach into his stock of memories from Russia and recreate an old one, and his productions of *The Nutcracker, Raymonda, Swan Lake, Sleeping Beauty,* and *Don Quixote* have spanned the globe. But they are never museum pieces or creaky vehicles for an egotistical star. Nureyev invariably brings his own, often controversial interpretation to these ballets, whether he is performing in someone else's "traditional" production or in his own.

Seeing the same role done by different dancers is part of the fascination of ballet. If you have seen Nureyev's Siegfried in *Swan Lake,* not for a moment have you seen all Siegfrieds, for Baryshnikov's, Dowell's, Lavrovsky's, and Cragun's interpretations, among others, are still worth seeing, so different and revealing are the performances of these various dancers. That Nureyev is preferred, that his single name in an otherwise unknown production can sell out the theater, is perhaps the supreme compliment that his public can pay him.

But Nureyev brings more to his performances than his individual qualities as a dancer. His presence in any role, of course, is a very potent force on any stage, something that the nineteenth-century choreographers who originally created these parts did not have to work with, in that age when few talented men were taking dancing seriously as a career. When he is criticized for tampering with the classics, his reply is that we dance these ballets *now,* and should make use of our modern resources of technique and insight. The power of his name—and the expectation of seeing him perform his pyrotechnics—have brought vast audiences to the ballet, people who might not otherwise have dreamed of spending an evening at *Swan Lake* or *Giselle.*

Since his early years in Russia—years of poverty, wartime shortages, the meager meals of boiled potatoes—Nureyev has had to rely on his intelligence and strong sense of self-preservation. Born in 1938 near Irkutsk, which borders on Mongolia, he is the son of a career military man and his wife, both Tatars. Of

Preceding pages: *Nureyev in* Swan Lake. Top left: *Nureyev's first American TV appearance, in Bournonville's* Flower Festival Pas de Deux. Top right: *With Bruhn and Gregory after* Raymonda. Above: *As Siegfried in the Kirov's* Swan Lake.

Fonteyn and Nureyev, one of the great partnerships of modern ballet. Below: *Rehearsing Act II of* Giselle, *the first ballet of their partnership.* Right: *In John Neumeier's* Don Juan. *Bottom left: In the title roles of Sir Frederick Ashton's* Marguerite and Armand, *based on Dumas's* Lady of the Camellias. *Bottom right: In the tomb scene from Kenneth MacMillan's* Romeo and Juliet.

his ancestry Nureyev has written, "Tatars are quick to catch fire, quick to get into a fight, unassuming, yet at the same time passionate and sometimes as cunning as a fox. The Tatar is in fact a pretty complex animal." That is an effective description of Nureyev himself.

The war years were hard on his family, and basics such as food and shelter were hard to come by. His father was often away for long periods of time, and young Nureyev, with his mother and sisters, moved frequently and lived in claustrophobic quarters, often with strangers. His earliest cultural experience was listening to the family radio, which occasionally abandoned its standard programming of popular music—much to Nureyev's delight—for works by Russian composers such as Tchaikovsky and Borodin.

His first ballet experience came in 1945 when the entire family managed to sneak into the Bashkir Opera and Ballet Theater on a single ticket. The ballet was *Song of the Cranes,* based on Bashkir legend, and it set Nureyev on his career. He learned the rudiments of ballet in his hometown of Ufa from the seventy-year-old dancer Udeltsova, who had once been a member of Diaghilev's company. She encouraged him to study at the Vaganova Choreographic Institute in Leningrad (formerly the Imperial School of St. Petersburg, where Nijinsky had studied and danced for the greater glory of the czar; the school is still the finest in the world). But Leningrad was a thousand miles away, and Nureyev might as well have wished for the moon.

Nevertheless, by a combination of persistence, luck, and daring, by 1955 he was taking his entrance examinations at the Institute—at the age of seventeen already considerably older than the usual age for application. "Young man," he was told, "you'll either become a brilliant dancer or a total failure—and most likely you'll be a failure." Since Nureyev had already acquired considerable dancing experience at the opera house in Ufa, he regarded this as a challenge. He succeeded in being admitted into the classes of Alexander Pushkin, one of the Institute's foremost teachers. His demand for perfection and the speed with which he learned his roles brought his extraordinary talent to the attention of the faculty, though he also won the dislike of his fellow students because he had not worked his way up in the ordinary way. As a result of his performance at the Moscow competition of 1958, he was offered a contract with the Kirov Ballet.

Just three years later, he cut short his association with the company, by defecting during its 1961 Paris–London tour. His break did not come as a complete surprise to his fellow dancers: he had always been rebellious and individualistic, refusing to be regimented into the Komsomol, a student organization that prepares its members for entry into the Communist party; and he has always been inquisitive about what was happening else-

where in the world, particularly in the world of ballet. Aware that they had a maverick in their midst, the Soviet authorities frequently sent him out of Leningrad when visiting companies from the West were scheduled to appear there. On one such occasion, the danseur noble Erik Bruhn (who was one of Nureyev's early champions and later one of his closest friends) was appearing with American Ballet Theatre; Nureyev was so anxious to see him that he left a movie camera with a friend to record the famous Dane's performances, so that he could see them when he returned to Leningrad after his own tour.

However, circumstance had played into Nureyev's hands more than once, and he was always quick to seize momentary advantages. Such an occasion came during the Kirov's 1961 tour. While in Paris, Nureyev characteristically broke company rules; he stayed out late, savoring new friends, Parisian nightlife, and his newfound popularity. He realized that he would probably never be allowed to leave the USSR again; moreover, he might be forced out of the Kirov. The company was due to fly on to London; but when the Soviet authorities attempted to seize him at the airport to send him back to Moscow, he found the courage to escape them and throw himself into the arms of the airport police—in a moment abandoning homeland, family, and relative security to make an uncertain career in the West.

Nureyev says that his decision was not political; he had tasted personal and artistic freedom and acclaim, and he simply wanted more. His dramatic defection established him as a dashing figure whom the public would want to see live up to a glamorous reputation. He was young, attractive, flamboyant, temperamental—though much later he commented to Margot Fonteyn that "I do not have courage to be as wicked as I want"; he seemed to court scandal, and during his early years the papers zeroed in on his wildness, turning incidents into explosions. But Nureyev has never had a press agent, has never sought publicity for its own sake. In 1961, as now, he was interested only in the achievement of excellence in his dancing and in finding opportunities to perform a wide variety of roles.

Today, when defections have become almost commonplace—Natalia Makarova and Mikhail Baryshnikov are among those who have now established major careers in the West—Nureyev almost seems part of the dance Establishment, despite his reputation for rebelliousness. But in 1961 it remained to be proved that he was not merely an exotic flash in the pan. His first performances in Paris had been condemned by no less a personage than Serge Lifar, director of the Paris Opera Ballet. "Unstable, hysterical, and vain," wrote Lifar. "He is simply a boy who stood against discipline, necessary in all art. This discipline is work, not whiskey at five o'clock in the morning. Now he betrays the whole world." Lifar's opinions were shared by a great many critics—Communist and non-Communist alike—

Left: *Nureyev in the title role of John Neumeier's* Don Juan, *with the National Ballet of Canada.* Above, *from left to right: David Wall, Nureyev, Ann Jenner, and Anthony Dowell in the Royal Ballet's production of* Dances at a Gathering, *choreographed by Jerome Robbins.*

who were appalled by what they considered to be Nureyev's irresponsibility in deserting the company that had trained and supported him. During those early months, Nureyev was under tremendous political pressure to return to Russia; at one performance in France, local Communists littered the stage with broken glass.

With no Diaghilev to sponsor and shape his career and give him the performing base and creative opportunities that every great dancer needs, Nureyev set out to conquer the Western dance world alone. Within a week he made his first appearance with a Western company, the International Ballet of the Marquis de Cuevas, alternately performing as Prince Florimund and as the Bluebird in a production of *Sleeping Beauty* that he did not particularly like. Soon he traveled to Copenhagen to meet Erik Bruhn, a man ten years his senior, who has exerted considerable influence on Nureyev's dancing. Nureyev regarded Bruhn as the greatest dancer he had seen and the only one whom he felt was worthy of emulation. While in Copenhagen, he studied the Bournonville technique, so carefully preserved by the Royal Danish Ballet, and he also took classes with Vera Volkova, a prominent Russian teacher. Through Volkova, Nureyev met the Royal Ballet's prima ballerina, Margot Fonteyn, and this resulted in two of the most famous partnerships of our time: Nureyev and Fonteyn, Nureyev and the Royal Ballet.

Fonteyn had danced her first *Swan Lake* the year Nureyev was born; she was already something of an institution in British ballet when the twenty-four-year-old Nureyev arrived on the scene. "Rudolf Nureyev brought me a second career, like Indian Summer," Fonteyn wrote over a decade later in her autobiography. But she did not dance with him at the beginning of his association with the Royal Ballet; rather, she arranged for his English stage debut at a benefit for the Royal Academy of Dance (associated with the Royal Ballet), in a short and stormy solo choreographed for him by Sir Frederick Ashton to Scriabin's *Poème Tragique*. This was followed by a pas de deux performed with Rosella Hightower. Nureyev was an instant success, and the occasion of his debut with Fonteyn in *Giselle* shortly afterward was a much-publicized event.

The Covent Garden debut with Fonteyn in 1962 met with mixed critical notices: many protests came from critics who did not approve of Nureyev's interpolations for Albrecht in the second act. Although making changes proved to be a trademark of Nureyev's work with other classics, the traditionally conservative balletomanes found them disruptive—and to some extent, still do. But the changes seem to be made with an eye toward two goals: giving more dancing to the male lead, and making the classics more dramatically palatable. In most cases, they are effective.

Nureyev came to assimilate much of the softer English style in his dancing, while imparting something of the fiery, spirited Russian style to other dancers. His unusual ability to assume not only his own role, but to learn all the other dancing roles as well, has given him the ability to create a production that was a harmonious whole, not just a showcase for star performers. This overview, combined with his attention to details, makes him a sharp and much-needed critic of British ballet.

There was never serious discussion about his becoming a permanent member of the British company, and Nureyev's peripatetic life-style, which is still one of his most visible offstage characteristics, exerted itself too frequently for him to be able to put down roots in England. But the Royal Ballet's founder-director, Dame Ninette de Valois, offered him her full support, and Nureyev has frequently performed as a guest artist with the company ever since.

Nureyev has partnered most of the world's ranking ballerinas: the Royal Ballet's Antoinette Sibley and Merle Park, Natalia Makarova, Carla Fracci, and American Ballet Theatre's Cynthia Gregory, to name only a few. But his partnership with Fonteyn was, and on rare occasions still is, something magical. Neither dancer can account for their incredible affinity. Fonteyn marvels at photographs that show their heads tilted at precisely complementary angles that just "happened" without being planned. His presentation of her as his ballerina displayed a passionate solicitude that hinted at a visceral rapport beyond words. In the great classical roles they danced together, from their first *Giselle* at Covent Garden in 1961 to *Swan Lake* and *Sleeping Beauty* soon after, his dramatic interpretations were in keeping with his philosophy that classical ballet need not emasculate or subordinate the male. When he danced with Fonteyn, and to a somewhat lesser extent with his other partners, it was never less than a love duet, and her cool British understatement took fire from his Dionysian approach to dance. If the audience was more than usually aware of the danseur's presence in a pas de deux, it did not detract from Fonteyn but gave her the added dimension of being seen through an adoring "lover's" eyes. The sexual balance between the danseur and the ballerina was restored, and passion, more than a little stirred by Nureyev's sheer animal magnetism, took the stage.

Aside from the classics, the two ballets most closely associated with their partnership are Ashton's *Marguerite and Armand*, created for them in 1963 and never performed by any other dancers, and Kenneth MacMillan's full-length *Romeo and Juliet*, choreographed by MacMillan for the young British dancers Lynn Seymour and Christopher Gable, but actually premiered by Fonteyn and Nureyev in 1964. *Marguerite and Armand*, a one-act retelling of the story of *The Lady of the Camellias*, set to Liszt's Piano Sonata in B-minor, is not a virtuoso

Nureyev with Lynn Seymour in Glen Tetley's modern ballet Laborintus.

Above: *Nureyev as Balanchine's Prodigal Son, stripped of his possessions, in performance with the Royal Ballet.* Opposite: *In Rudi van Dantzig's* The Ropes of Time.

showpiece for its stars, though Ashton conceived it as a vehicle for their personalities: for Fonteyn's womanly vulnerability and Nureyev's "dynamism, his romantic qualities and his acting ability." Nureyev's romantic dash and penchant for sweeping gestures have seldom found richer outlet for expression. His headlong entrance with his cloak billowing behind him at the close of Marguerite's fatal interview with Armand's father is an unforgettable image of youthful ardor. French ballerina Violette Verdy, a close observer of Nureyev, has further articulated his aesthetic sense for things romantic: "Rudi can arrive at great essential moments of classical, romantic suggestions about another world, about fairy tales, about ballet, about dance, about the male in dance. I think that he is at his best here—symbolically, he becomes very beautiful and rich. We see him within his great background and his great schooling."

She might have said much the same of Nureyev's performance in that quintessentially romantic ballet, *Romeo and Juliet*. Kenneth MacMillan's version of the work, along with Fonteyn's and Nureyev's performance in the leading roles, is known to millions, not only through live performance but through the popular film made of the Royal Ballet's production in 1966. This was Nureyev's second film appearance (his first was in *An Evening with the Royal Ballet*), and though he was not altogether pleased with the results, claiming that the camera tended to cut off a hand or some other extremity at the apex of a grand jeté, we are nevertheless grateful to have this brilliant record of a great dancer at the height of his powers—of Nijinsky, for example, we are left with virtually nothing. Perhaps wishing to be well remembered by posterity, Nureyev has had a major hand in making two subsequent films in which he has starred: *I Am a Dancer* (1972), which contains his performance with Fonteyn in *Marguerite and Armand,* excerpts from other works, and some class and rehearsal and other candid footage; and the full-length classic *Don Quixote,* which he coproduced in 1972. But *Romeo and Juliet,* probably the most popular ballet in the Royal Ballet's repertoire, is probably also the most popular work in Nureyev's.

The film of *Romeo and Juliet* still turns up regularly in movie theaters and on television in New York and other cities. If Nureyev could perform the role of Romeo every night—an effort that would certainly tax even his legendary stamina—he would undoubtedly fill the opera house of almost any major city. Why? Because in this ballet, Shakespeare's love story is wedded to Prokofiev's passionate score, and Fonteyn and Nureyev make their bodies sing, from their introduction as reckless young lovers, to the ecstatic sweep of the Balcony Scene Pas de Deux, to the final agony in the tomb, when Romeo desperately attempts to partner a seemingly lifeless Juliet. What we respond to here is the elemental power of the emotions the

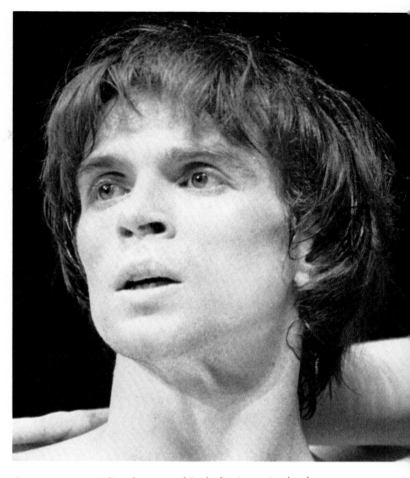

dancers portray, riding the crest of Prokofiev's music, the thrust of MacMillan's choreography. Fonteyn has made the role of Juliet peculiarly her own, convincing her audiences time and again that she is a young girl awaking to her sensuality; the role seems to be one of the last she is willing to relinquish in the twilight of her career. Nureyev has performed Romeo with other ballerinas, including Lynn Seymour, but it is with Fonteyn that the transcendent magic of great partnership, so essential and appropriate to this ballet, occurs. The role of Romeo, with its magnificent opportunities for solo dancing, pas de deux, and intense characterization, is one of the most coveted in the modern repertoire, and it was one of the first parts that Mikhail Baryshnikov essayed when he made his initial appearances as a guest artist with the Royal Ballet. But those Romeos have fared best who have performed in great partnerships: Christopher Gable with Lynn Seymour, Anthony Dowell with Antoinette Sibley and Natalia Makarova, and Richard Cragun with Marcia Haydée in John Cranko's version for the Stuttgart Ballet.

Surprisingly few roles have been created for Nureyev since he came to the West, and he himself has choreographed only one entirely original ballet, the short-lived *Tancredi,* to a score

129

by Hans Werner Henze in Vienna in 1966. *Tancredi*'s score was written in the early 1950s for a ballet by Victor Gsovsky, which was not successful; the score, with libretto by Peter Csobadi, was offered to Nureyev as a package. It was not, then, a collaborative project from the beginning, and it has been suggested that this might have been partially responsible for some of the difficulties it presented in production. It deals with a theme that was certainly familiar to Nureyev from his dancing of *Swan Lake:* the antithetical pulls of sacred and profane—or physical—love. In the course of this work, however, he did create some demandingly athletic ensembles for male dancers, as well as creating the central role, that of Tancredi, to suit his own talents as a danseur.

Nureyev and Fonteyn began a mutual exploration of a more modern idiom in *Paradise Lost* (1966) and *Pelleas and Melisande* (1968), choreographed for them by Roland Petit. Ever seeking to widen his dance horizons, Nureyev began to dance the repertoire of the Dutch choreographer Rudi van Dantzig, appearing in his *Monument for a Dead Boy* with the Dutch National Ballet during the 1968–1969 season; in 1970 van Dantzig choreographed *Ropes of Time* for Nureyev and the Royal Ballet. Nureyev was, in fact, much responsible for bringing the breath of modernism to the Royal, first in the rather unsuccessful Petit experiments with Fonteyn, and later with van Dantzig and Glen Tetley, who created *Field Figures* for the Royal in 1970 and *Laborintus* for Nureyev and the company in 1971. Nureyev had not only given his adopted company his staging of classics such as *La Bayadère,* the pas de deux from *Le Corsaire,* the third act of *Raymonda,* and his full-length *Nutcracker;* he challenged them to look to the future of dance, himself acting as the bridge between two very different disciplines and ranging ever farther afield in his search for new material to master.

His first performance in a modern dance work came when he appeared with the Paul Taylor Company during its 1971–1972 season, performing Taylor's own role in his *Aureole* and in his *Book of Beasts.* In 1974, the great modern dance choreographer Martha Graham remarked of Nureyev: "He doesn't permit himself to be limited. . . . He wants to break the mold that the audiences have made for him to move into twentieth-century things. . . . I've been rehearsing with Rudolf and he has an endless capacity for work." In 1975, Graham choreographed her modern *Lucifer* and then *The Scarlet Letter* for him. He has also appeared in two Graham classics, as the Revivalist in *Appalachian Spring* and Oedipus in *Night Journey.*

This "endless capacity" remarked upon by Graham is not idle hyperbole; it is fact. An article in the *New York Times* in 1975 summarized the staggering schedule of six weeks in the

Perhaps the most noteworthy of Nureyev's forays into the modern dance repertoire has been his association with Martha Graham. He is seen here in several Graham works. Opposite: *With Diane Gray in* Night Journey, *based on the myth of Oedipus.* Top: *As the Revivalist, a role created in 1944 by Merce Cunningham, in* Appalachian Spring. Above: *As Arthur Dimmesdale, with Bonnie Oda Homsey as Pearl (left) and Janet Eilber as Hester Prynne, in* The Scarlet Letter, *a dance Graham created for Nureyev in 1975.*

danseur's life. In one week, Nureyev danced three performances in New York of the full-length *Raymonda,* which he had recently restaged for American Ballet Theatre; then he spent two weeks in Washington, where he performed four demanding ballets each evening for twelve performances in a row —a schedule that would have been killing for a member of a corps de ballet, never mind a principal dancer. He followed this with eighteen performances, over a three-week period, with the National Ballet of Canada. Further insight into the rigors of Nureyev's self-imposed discipline is evident in the evening-length Broadway engagement called ''Nureyev and Friends,'' which was deliberately programmed to display the range of the dancer's skills: there were thirty-four performances of the same four ballets (by Balanchine, Bournonville, Taylor, and Limón), with Nureyev dancing in every ballet at every performance. Another source reported that Nureyev was ''in his fourteenth week of nonstop dancing with five companies on two continents and only one foot is injured and bandaged.''

Nureyev adapted his dancing to that particular injury, he says, by doing double tours by going up from the flat foot instead of from demi-pointe. But aside from the danger of dancing with an injured foot, he sometimes brings criticism on himself from the uncomprehending, who fear that he may be overdancing, driving himself on a suicidal course that will result in an early end to his career. In defiance of their prophecies, Nureyev claims that he dances best when he is tired and his muscles are thoroughly warm—and he does seem to thrive on the demands he makes of himself. He bounces back from frequent injury with altogether inhuman speed—or dances on, regardless. In fact, he has noticeably improved with time, bringing a deeper maturity to his interpretations and endowing his dancing with a golden quality, which could only be gained from years of work and carefully considered experience.

A dancer's career is comparatively short, and by the time he reaches forty he has usually passed the peak of physical prowess and must adapt to the process of aging. The age at which this occurs is not the same for all dancers, of course; Murray Louis claims that he never danced better than when he passed forty; but the change that takes place is inevitable. Nureyev's fearsome activity is a reply to this inevitability.

There are dancers, younger men such as Baryshnikov and Bujones, who have already begun to lay claim to Nureyev's laurels. But Nureyev is philosophical about that. ''I have taken myself out of races a long time ago,'' he remarks with calm assurance; and not feeling the need to compete, he has been able to concentrate on that single objective, perfecting his art. Not feeling the need to compete, he is always ready to help another dancer. His advent at the Royal Ballet may have been a mixed blessing, since it robbed other dancers of both spotlight

and performances. Yet Anthony Dowell, a member of the corps de ballet when Nureyev came on the scene in 1962 and now the company's resident premier danseur, credits Nureyev's influence and active help in forming his technique. There is no doubt that Nureyev has had a galvanizing effect on British male dancing; or that, wherever he goes, whether as dancer or as régisseur, his example and high standards effect transformations in many of the dancers he works with. His partnership with Karen Kain of the National Ballet of Canada has made her something of an international star, and though his close ties with that company have been criticized by nationalistic Canadians who feel that his roles should be danced by regular members of the company, his appearances with the Canadians have made possible their annual tours to New York and the glamor and new prestige that result from international as opposed to provincial status.

It would seem that Nureyev has all a man could want. He reportedly earns about $4,000 a performance, often more (though often less, if he particularly covets a role or wishes to help a friend); some of the material symbols of his affluence include a villa in the south of France and the furs and other exotic, expensive clothing he favors offstage. He has a consuming interest in his profession and is at the top of it. Very few dancers, for example, could have filled the Uris Theatre on Broadway for five weeks, aided by only a few of his friends. Clive Barnes has suggested that Isadora Duncan could have, and Pavlova, Martha Graham, and Nijinsky. But Nureyev's is the only other name one could add with assurance to the list.

On the other hand, his professed ambition of dancing with Balanchine has so far been denied him—"Come back when you are tired of playing the prince," Balanchine is reported to have told him when Nureyev explored the possibility of assuming a relationship with the New York City Ballet in the early 1960s. But in the years since, he has appeared in two of the greatest roles that Balanchine created for the male dancer, in his *Apollo* and in *Prodigal Son*.

What is it like to be Rudolf Nureyev, to live out of a suitcase (he was actually born on a train, and wanderlust seems to be in his blood), taking planes as routinely as other people take the bus, spending almost every waking moment either preparing for a performance—in class, in rehearsal—or winding down from it? "You feel like cattle before the slaughter, and there is no escape. . . . Really, what it all boils down to is that we are paid for our fear. . . . My whole life is about being on the stage," he said recently in an interview with dance writer John Gruen. To be Rudolf Nureyev is to dance in frequent pain, with constant fear; to perform before audiences that have been learning over the years to judge danseurs by the standards he established; to enter each night into a modern gladiatorial arena.

He is known as one of ballet's keenest critics, with the kind of acute perception that is unexpected in one so deeply involved in the field. He constantly turns this critical eye inward. His close friend, the danseur Erik Bruhn, tells of one particularly brilliant performance given by Nureyev in which he missed a single step, unknown to the audience or other dancers. Although Nureyev did not show his distress to the public, according to Bruhn, his evening was ruined and he spent a sleepless night, worried and upset. Such self-criticism is rare, especially in one at the pinnacle of his profession, as is Nureyev.

Has his full potential ever been realized? Very little has actually been choreographed for Nureyev, perhaps because of his own strong opinions, perhaps because no choreographer alive today is able to use his gifts to best advantage. It has been speculated that Balanchine might have been such a mentor, had the two men been able to come to a meeting of minds. Violette Verdy, for many years a leading ballerina with the New York City Ballet and now director of the Paris Opera Ballet, has said: "I feel that Nureyev is such a great artist and dancer that only men like Balanchine and Robbins . . . could have used Rudi to the full measure of his talent—used him, and been able to challenge him. . . . We haven't seen what Rudolf can do because he has never been challenged."

To be the most famous dancer in the world—which Nureyev certainly is—is not necessarily to be the best, in this age of mass media and publicity. Yet there is solid achievement behind Nureyev's glittering reputation and the almost hysterical audience reaction to his performances. Nureyev has often been compared with Nijinsky, and points of comparison certainly do exist. However, the art that Nijinsky served is separated from Nureyev's by half a century, during which time astonishing changes have taken place—including the development of motion pictures, television, and rapid transportation—that have exposed Nureyev to greater pressures, larger audiences, and higher public standards of dance than Nijinsky could have dreamed of. That Nureyev probably has a better technique than Nijinsky had is generally accepted, since teaching methods have improved, and the choreographic explorations of Nijinsky's day have been absorbed into the mainstream of ballet today, giving the male dancer a wider range of challenging movement.

Nijinsky succumbed to the pressures of a world gone mad with war and mechanization; Nureyev from his earliest hungry years in Russia has been a survivor, whose determination has enraged and delighted governments, fellow dancers, critics, and would-be friends. He has not allowed himself to be discouraged by setbacks or consumed by the outstanding success of his numerous accomplishments, and he has pursued unwaveringly a single course: the achievement of excellence in dance.

Opposite top: *Nureyev taking class, the daily ritual of every dancer.* Opposite bottom: *Nureyev on the go, after receiving the Dance Magazine Award in 1973*

133

7

A
Contemporary
Galaxy

Today, dancers routinely venture into new terrain and try new techniques, making guest appearances or performing special seasons with a freedom formerly unknown. In America what began with television programs such as the "Bell Telephone Hour," which brought Nureyev, Bruhn, d'Amboise, and Villella before the eyes of a mass audience, continues today with the series "Dance in America," which has presented everything from the Romantic *Les Sylphides* to the stark, modern works of Merce Cunningham. On commercial television, the Bolshoi's full-length *Romeo* made it possible for Mikhail Lavrovsky's dancing to be seen by numbers unimaginable in the time of Pavlova, however often Pavlova may have sailed in search of new audiences for ballet.

Who is the greatest danseur today? This question, so often asked, is difficult to answer without a multitude of qualifications. No two men perform exactly the same roles, nor do they have the same opportunities to work with choreographers who will extend their technique; and it is nearly impossible to make an exact comparison of their achievements.

For the classics, Denmark's Erik Bruhn was for a time without peer. He emerged in the 1950s as the leading danseur noble of his generation, in roles such as Albrecht, Siegfried, and James, and performed his heritage of Bournonville dance with verve and ballon. Some of his audience found him cold and detached and thought his technique was too effortless—some of the same criticisms now leveled at Mikhail Baryshnikov and Fernando Bujones. Yet that same control could smolder and take fire in dramatic roles: it appeared as suppressed passion in Birgit Cullberg's dance adaptation of Strindberg's *Miss Julie*, in which the butler Jean turns and destroys his teasing mistress; it became macho passion in Roland Petit's *Carmen* and full-blown lust in MacMillan's brooding *Las Hermanas,* based on the play by Federico Garcia Lorca.

Bruhn's consideration of his partners, from Alicia Markova to Carla Fracci to Natalia Makarova, was legendary. Though he made his career more in the limelight that American Ballet Theatre could offer him than in his homeland, consequently becoming much better known internationally than his compatriots Henning Kronstam and Niels Kehlet, Bruhn is nevertheless much honored in Denmark and has occasionally appeared with the Royal Danish Ballet. Plagued by injury and illness, he cut short his dancing career in 1972. But in 1975, past the age of forty, he returned to the stage, announcing his intention to explore new material rather than attempting to equal past performances. Since then he has performed roles—in John Neumeier's *Epilogue* and Nureyev's *Raymonda*—that were choreographed for the "new" Erik Bruhn, a dancer who admits to technical limitations that come inevitably with age, but who still has much to give an audience. Few of his new roles have offered him the opportunity for virtuosic display, with the exception of the pas de trois from Bournonville's *La Ventana,* which he staged for himself with Cynthia Gregory and Rudolf Nureyev; but he has nevertheless been magnificent in such parts as Petrouchka or The Man She Must Marry in Tudor's *Lilac Garden.* And in the hands of such an experienced and resourceful actor, mime roles such as Madge in *La Sylphide* and Dr. Coppelius can steal the show.

Denmark may be a small country, but it looms large in the dance world. The high-flying joie de vivre that characterizes the Bournonville style, lovingly preserved in the repertoire of the Royal Danish Ballet since the nineteenth century, has recommended danseurs such as Borge Ralov, Fredbjorn Bjornsson, Henning Kronstam, Niels Kehlet, Flemming Flindt, and the young Ib Anderson to an international audience. In the 1940s, the company's virtuosity and mastery of classical technique was displayed in Harold Lander's popular ballet *Etudes,* which begins with young students demonstrating the five positions. The ballet escalates to the tune of orchestrated piano exercises through barre work and adagio, to a dizzying, pyrotechnical finale. The work remains in the Danish repertoire as a continu-

136

Preceding pages: *Gary Chryst, Christian Holder, and Dermot Burke in Gerald Arpino's rock ballet* Trinity, *the signature work of The Joffrey Ballet.*
Above: *Erik Bruhn and Carla Fracci in the Balcony Scene from* Romeo and Juliet.

ing challenge to each succeeding generation of dancers.

The Royal Danish Ballet first went on international tour in the early 1950s and has been increasingly familiar on ballet circuits since. In 1966, the directorship of the company was taken over by the dancer and choreographer Flemming Flindt, who has expanded the repertoire beyond Bournonville and other classics to include avant-garde, highly theatrical works, such as his own *Triumph of Death* (1972). One might imagine that the director of one of the world's leading ballet companies would be a staid individual. But Flindt shattered that stereotype with his dance version of the Ionesco-based shocker *The Lesson,* in which he performed the role of a homicidal ballet teacher; in *Triumph of Death* he appears in the nude, covered with reddish paint! The Danish audience has largely accepted his innovations, which have included bringing modern dance by such choreographers as Paul Taylor and Murray Louis into the company repertoire. In 1976, Flindt announced that he would resign, in 1978, in order to freelance as a choreographer. It will be difficult to replace him. Among his potential successors, the name most often heard is that of Peter Martins, the young Dane who, since 1969, has made his career as a principal dancer with the New York City Ballet.

In the absence of Edward Villella—who after many injuries has virtually retired from the stage—and Jacques d'Amboise—who performs less and less often—Martins has emerged as the New York City Ballet's leading danseur, most often in partnership with Suzanne Farrell. Martins's dancing is elegant and long-limbed; his Danish classical training has equipped him well for the intricacies and speed required in Balanchine's neoclassical ballets. He is not the first danseur from Denmark to find a niche with the NYCB nor is he even the most recent; Bruhn spent several seasons with the company, performing in such ballets as *Theme and Variations* and *La Sonnambula,* and Peter Schaufuss, son of the Royal Danish Ballet's Frank Schaufuss, joined the company in 1974. But Martins has spent some of his formative years as an artist working with Balanchine, and the two share a mutual respect; Martins has been one of the few dancers entrusted with the responsibility—and honor—of teaching company class in Balanchine's absence.

One of the ballet's most striking danseurs nobles, with his tall, elegant body and handsome head, Martins is an excellent partner who takes a keen interest in complementing and presenting the ballerina, whether she is Suzanne Farrell, the more petite and spicy Kay Mazzo, or another dancer from the company. But he has said that he is bored with the idea of always playing the prince, and an occasional appearance with the Danes—in *La Sylphide,* for example—or in Balanchine's version of the second act of *Swan Lake,* or in his restaging of *Coppélia,* appears to satisfy his appetite for the nineteenth-

century repertoire. Of what he has learned at the New York City Ballet, Martins has said: "I always thought of myself as a pure classical dancer. But then suddenly dance became unlimited to me. That's basically why I'm still with the company." With two of the world's greatest choreographers—Balanchine and Robbins—creating new roles for him (an opportunity that, for all his achievements as a dancer, Bruhn was denied in his career), Martins seems in little hurry to accept any offer, however flattering, to move on. He could become a superstar; he could command high fees; he was even invited to take over the Royal Danish Ballet from Flindt.

Yet Martins is a dancer with an eye to the future, one who is already preparing for the time when he will no longer be able to dance. In 1977, he took his first steps as a choreographer with *Calcium Night Light,* a solo he created for a fellow member of the City Ballet, Daniel Duell. He produced the ballet himself, as part of an evening of NYCB dancers presented at Brooklyn College. Brilliant dancer, occasional teacher, budding choreographer, and fledgling impresario, Martins has the attributes for a long and important career in dance.

Peter Martins is one of several European-trained danseurs who have been willing to make the full commitment required of any dancer who joins the New York City Ballet. With Jean-Pierre Bonnefous from France, Danish-trained Helgi Tomasson from Iceland, and his compatriot Peter Schaufuss, Martins alternates roles in the company's repertoire, which is designed primarily to display the choreographic gifts of George Balanchine rather than the virtuosity or charisma of the company's dancers. These four danseurs, who might have become stars in their native lands, have instead freely chosen to submerge their personalities in exchange for the artistic satisfaction of working with Balanchine—one of the great choreographers of our time—and Jerome Robbins. What of the dancers who have come up through the New York City Ballet's school and organization?

Edward Villella, perhaps the most popular and best-known danseur America has produced, is a tireless proselytizer for public acceptance of the virility of the danseur. But he has scarcely danced with his home company for several seasons. The roles he made his own over the years—Balanchine's *Prodigal Son,* for example—as well as the parts he created in such ballets as *Tarantella, Jewels,* and *Bugaku,* have yet to be performed by other dancers with quite the virile excitement and panache that were his trademarks as an artist.

As a child, Villella, like most American boys, channeled his abundant physical energy into sports, until he discovered the tremendous freedom and exhilaration that he could achieve through the discipline of dance. "Male dancing borders on athleticism and on poetic qualities," he has written. "That's the

Opposite: *Three representatives of Danish ballet.* Top left: *Bruhn with Natalia Makarova in Neumeier's* Epilogue. Top right: *Flemming Flindt in his* Triumph of Death. Bottom: *Henning Kronstam as the professor in Flindt's* The Lesson.

main challenge: to have that marvelous virility and at the same time . . . move in a beautiful manner. Masculinity in dance is a fantastic attack and at the same time a delicate restraint. The difficulty is to control the attack.'' After a youthful period of flinging himself around the stage like a human dynamo, Villella went back to the beginnings of his technique and retaught himself how to stand, how to walk across the stage; he learned to control his strength and his movements. Reveling in his male technique, in the speed, weight, and power, in the height of his great jumps, which are the goals of most men in ballet, he also deeply appreciates the experience of partnering, of sensing the needs of another body: ''The man does not just take an object and balance it. He takes a live individual and finds where her balance is; he anticipates her blur, putting her line back into focus and making it clear. I glory in partnering'' (*Dance Perspectives,* no. 40). Ballerinas such as the New York City Ballet's Patricia McBride, with whom he was often teamed, could testify to that.

From the dynamo of *Tarantella* to the contemplative figure of *Watermill,* a mysterious, slow-moving revery created by Jerome Robbins for Villella in 1972, he proved to be a danseur who thinks about his art, who causes others to stop and consider the man who dances. As Villella has said, ''It's so much more than the athlete approaching the ball with a bat; he can

accomplish his feats in any way best suited to him. The dancer has to accomplish his feats within the framework of a technique, a musical phrase, or a dramatic idea. He has to make them alive and beautiful.'' In his occasional guest appearances, in lecture demonstrations, and in his own choreography for television—*Dance of the Athletes,* for example—Villella is trying to express this vision of dance, its form and substance and its physical satisfactions for a man.

Villella and Jacques d'Amboise both have had much to do in recent years with reshaping American ideas of men in dance. D'Amboise had been a principal dancer with the New York City Ballet for only a short while when he took his dance training to Hollywood in 1954. He appeared in several films, notably *Seven Brides for Seven Brothers,* a spirited musical about a family of young pioneers that contained important sequences of energetic, balletlike choreography. Reaching a mass audience through these films, d'Amboise had a major impact on the American idea of the male dancer; he helped to shape a new image of the danseur as an all-American boy. That done, he returned in 1956 to his first love, ballet, and to the New York City Ballet, which has been his haven ever since, however often he has ventured into television or guest appearances with other companies.

By 1957 (when he was twenty-three), he was performing

140

Above *and* opposite: *Peter Martins, a leading danseur with the New York City Ballet, rehearsing the first ballet he has choreographed, a solo titled* Calcium Night Light, *with Daniel Duell, also of the NYCB.*

the title role in Balanchine's *Apollo.* "I knew that I was terrible in my first *Apollo,"* he has said, "and when Balanchine did not come to me and tell me so, did not *train* me in it, I realized that to be a dancer you must work as a dancer, not as a robot. I knew then that your teachers can teach you so much—but that the learning process is limitless." He has proved to be a good self-critic and the prophet of his own success. Balanchine has shown his appreciation of d'Amboise's contributions to the company as a dancer not only by setting a number of pivotal roles on him—in *Stars and Stripes, Jewels,* and *Who Cares?,* for example—but by encouraging him as a choreographer. Today, d'Amboise spends a good deal of his time encouraging the next generation of boys to dance.

Ballet has long been stigmatized by men in America as a "sissy," "elitist" art form, but as dance increases in popularity and our society relaxes its puritanical guard about male self-expression, more and more men are attracted to dance. Jacques d'Amboise wants to catch them young, expose them early, and eventually interest them in dancing professionally. Standards of male dancing are rising so rapidly that it is no longer enough just to be male (as it once was) in order to be accepted by a ballet school. He feels that if the number of men in dance is to be significantly and consistently increased, ballet companies must have a large reserve of boys enrolled in dance classes from which they can draw. What he began some years ago in an effort to interest his own two sons in ballet has developed into regular dance classes for boys that he teaches at several schools in New York City. He begins with jazz because it's easiest and quickest and he wants to get them moving. ("Are these boys going to go down to Capezio's and buy themselves tights? Hell, no.") Many prominent American danseurs began with jazz or tap lessons and soon felt the urge to explore other forms of

Above: *Edward Villella, a virtuoso technician and a skilled dancer-actor, in Jerome Robbins's* Watermill. *This is a meticulously paced, slow-moving work that draws its inspiration from Oriental theater.* Right: *Peter Martins, formerly of the Royal Danish Ballet, and his frequent partner, Suzanne Farrell, in Balanchine's* Chaconne *at the New York City Ballet.* Opposite bottom: *Martins and Kay Mazzo in Balanchine's* Duo Concertante.

142

Dancers of the New York City Ballet. Above: *Jacques d'Amboise and Melissa Hayden in George Balanchine's* Apollo, *from an NBC-TV production.* Above right: *Jean-Pierre Bonnefous in Balanchine's Bicentennial ballet,* Union Jack. Right: *Kay Mazzo, Jacques d'Amboise, and members of the company in* Union Jack. Opposite: *Helgi Tomasson in Jerome Robbins's* Dybbuk Variations.

dance. It's getting them moving that's important, d'Amboise believes, showing them the joy of hovering in the air, giving them an outlet for their natural exuberance that can also win them admiration. And then—who knows? Perhaps that boy in the corner over there is the next d'Amboise, lingering to go over the routine just one more time after class . . .

The rising expectations of men in dance are demonstrated graphically at the New York City Ballet. A company noted since its inception for its orientation to the ballerina, the NYCB now fields a contingent of strong male soloists, in addition to established principals such as d'Amboise, Anthony Blum, Martins, Bonnefous, and Tomasson. Bart Cook is one of the danseurs who are stepping into major roles—Balanchine has even given him a new solo in the revised version of *Square Dance,* a ballet

Above: *Robert Joffrey rehearses Robert Thomas and Charthel Arthur in his ballet* Remembrances, *while ballet master Scott Barnard looks on.* Opposite bottom left: *Luis Fuente as the Torchbearer in Gerald Arpino's athletic all-male ballet* Olympics. Opposite top right: *Fernando Bujones at age 16, rehearsing; since his teens, Bujones has been hailed as the young prodigy of American ballet.* Opposite bottom right: *Bujones in Anton Dolin's* Variations for Four *with American Ballet Theatre.*

147

148

Opposite top left: *Ivan Nagy, of American Ballet Theatre, supporting Natalia Makarova in Kenneth MacMillan's* Concerto. Opposite top right: *Lawrence Rhodes in Eliot Feld's* At Midnight, *danced to Mahler's* Four Rückert Lieder. *Opposite bottom left: Bart Cook, of the New York City Ballet, as a hen-pecked member of the audience at a Chopin recital acting out one of his fantasies, in Jerome Robbins's comic ballet* The Concert. *Opposite bottom right: Dermot Burke in Gerald Arpino's modern interpretation of an ancient myth,* Orpheus Times Light[2], *a production of The Joffrey Ballet. Above: Bart Cook relaxing during a rehearsal break.*

previously more noted for its female virtuosity. In the absence of Villella, Tomasson and young Victor Castelli have both essayed the title role in *Prodigal Son.* And ballets such as Balanchine's *Union Jack* would scarcely be possible did the company not have what is probably the strongest male ensemble it has ever had.

Another company with a strong record of fostering American male talent is The Joffrey Ballet, directed by Robert Joffrey and his associate Gerald Arpino, who is also the company's resident choreographer. Their choice of repertoire, based on a no-star policy that gives everyone in the company a wide variety of roles to dance, has offered unique opportunities both to the individual danseur and to the male ensemble. Joffrey's own career as a dancer was brief, but he packed a good deal of experience into it, performing not only with Roland Petit's Ballets de Paris but with the modern dance company of May O'Donnell, a disciple of Martha Graham. From the time he formed his first company in 1956, with six dancers who toured cross-country in a station wagon loaded with costumes and props, his eye for other dancers' talent has been sure: the choreographers Arpino and Glen Tetley were members of the original Robert Joffrey Ballet, and artists such as Lawrence Rhodes and Helgi Tomasson spent formative years with his company.

Today, probably the best-known male performer of The Joffrey is Gary Chryst, one of the finest character dancers America has produced. Like many other American danseurs, Chryst did not begin ballet training early; he did not even initially intend to enter ballet at all—he studied at New York's High School for the Performing Arts, where he intended to become an actor, until he became intrigued by the possibilities of expression in dance. His body is not built on the long and elegant lines of the classical danseur; he came to ballet in his teens, too late for his feet to be beautifully arched or routinely pointed in flight. But he is no mean technician and no mere mime: his roles range from the pathos of Petrouchka to the soaring energy of his part in Arpino's rock ballet *Trinity.* In addition to these, he is known for his interpretation of the Chinese Conjuror in Massine's *Parade,* his slinky, loathsome Profiteer in Kurt Jooss's great antiwar statement *The Green Table,* and his comic flair in ballets such as *Interplay* and Twyla Tharp's *Deuce Coupe.* In *Cakewalk,* his "Sleight of Feet" solo and demented cape wavings as Louis the Illusionist invariably bring roars of appreciation from the audience. He is an electric performer, and, like Nijinsky, he is at his best in an idiosyncratic role that requires a soloist's technique. He has that rare, indefinable charisma that rivets an audience's attention to whatever he does on stage.

Chryst is a star by spontaneous combustion, known to the dance world more by his own irrepressible gifts than by exten-

sive publicity. He performs in a company that has never brought in guest artists and has rarely acquired dancers from abroad; Christian Holder from Jamaica, Luis Fuente from Spain, and Tom Van Cauwenbergh from Belgium are exceptions. The Joffrey Ballet explores the choreographic possibilities for male dancers as soloists, rather than as partners or members of the corps, in ballets such as Arpino's all-male *Olympics* or *Orpheus Times Light* [2].

By contrast, in the more classically oriented companies, such as American Ballet Theatre, it is the "princes" who reign supreme: those danseurs who can lend both aristocratic presence, partnering ability, and technical authority to bread-and-butter ballets such as *Swan Lake* and *Giselle.* Such danseurs, however versatile they may be in other ballets, are established as stars by these major roles of the Romantic imagination.

Fernando Bujones, for instance, of Cuban extraction, is largely a product of Balanchine's School of American Ballet, though when the time came to choose a company—and Bujones, the *wunderkind* of American male dancing in the mid-1970s, had that choice—he chose the more eclectic repertoire of American Ballet Theatre. With a gold medal at the prestigious international dance competition in Varna, Bulgaria, just behind him in 1974, Bujones—with his perfect feet, extraordinary extension and elevation, and virtuoso technique—was well on his way to becoming a superstar. But at the very moment of his big breakthrough into the consciousness of the dance public, his career was dealt a blow by the arrival in the United States of Mikhail Baryshnikov, following his defection from the Kirov Ballet. Nurtured by the traditions and training that had produced Nijinsky, Baryshnikov at twenty-six was a more finished artist than Bujones, and his defection in Toronto and subsequent "disappearance" for a time into the Canadian wilderness were romantic and exciting. Bujones and even the less spectacular Hungarian defector, danseur noble Ivan Nagy (who like Baryshnikov also joined American Ballet Theatre), were temporarily cast into the shade in the glare of publicity that attended Baryshnikov's arrival.

Before his American debut and even before his defection, the word on Baryshnikov had been out: he had the mark of greatness. If his stage presence was not yet as rich and satisfying as Nureyev's or Bruhn's in the classical roles, his technique was seamless, and his style appeared effortless.

His claim that he had defected to the West in order to dance a wider variety of roles was quickly substantiated, though not always successfully: he was criticized for changing the choreography of the Green Skater in Ashton's *Les Patineurs;* and the speed and precision of Balanchine's *Theme and Variations* made it, he said, the hardest role he had ever danced to date. It was certainly one that he could not immediately master.

Opposite top: *Mikhail Baryshnikov and Merle Park of the Royal Ballet in Kenneth MacMillan's* Romeo and Juliet.
Opposite bottom: *"Misha" relaxing with a friend's dogs.*

But he has certainly had his share of triumphs since July of 1974. He stunned the public by his technical brilliance at his very first performance in America, *Giselle,* doing a series of desperate, skimming *brisés volés* diagonally across the stage in the second act, and then repeating the tour de force moments later. Westerners were accustomed to danseurs—even great ones, such as Nureyev—who made visible preparations for difficult steps, visible adjustments of line and balance upon landing from a combination in the air before going into the next movement. A certain amount of imperfection was accepted as inevitable, even exciting. But there was little, if any, of this with Baryshnikov. His combinations flowed one into the other with quicksilver ease, and his ballon was little short of miraculous. His training with Russia's great teacher, the late Alexander Pushkin, had made him the near-perfect instrument for classical dance.

Confronted for the first time in his life with complete freedom of decision in his choice of roles, he quickly added not only nineteenth-century works such as *La Sylphide* to his repertoire (he was coached in the role of James and in the alien Bournonville style by Erik Bruhn), but danced in a revival of Petit's *Le Jeune Homme et la Mort.* He essayed the role of The Boy with Matted Hair (created for Anthony Dowell) in Tudor's *Shadowplay* and had a major success in Fokine's *The Specter*

Baryshnikov at rehearsals for Eliot Feld's Variations on ''America.'' *Opposite: With Christine Sarry. Above: With Feld in the choreographer's studio. Left: At attention, in mid-air.*

of the Rose. A new generation of critics felt that to see him in this role was like seeing photographs of Nijinsky come to life.

Choreographers proved eager to work with him, and he with them. He had his first experience with modern ballet in John Butler's pas de deux *Medea,* which he danced at the 1975 Spoleto Festival with Carla Fracci. Twyla Tharp's *Push Comes to Shove,* which he first performed in 1976, was American Ballet Theatre's biggest hit in many years and helped to establish a new image for Baryshnikov: that of an impish, self-assured modern young man, so secure in his technique that he could afford to be self-mocking. He was irresistible, hilarious, deadpan, tossing off with nonchalance apparently impossible off-balance combinations that Tharp admits she could have created for no other artist. The ballet was possibly the greatest extension of Baryshnikov's dance vocabulary since he came to the West.

Like Nureyev, Baryshnikov has evinced an unwillingness to be tied down and an almost insatiable appetite for the international smorgasbord of new ballets and ballerinas to partner. Early in 1977 his freelance activities took him to the downtown New York studio of Eliot Feld to work with the choreographer on a new pas de deux for himself and ballerina Christine Sarry, *Variations on "America,"* performed during the Feld company's spring season in New York. It was their first collaboration, and the two men, almost the same age, found themselves to be kindred spirits. Baryshnikov threw himself into the tongue-in-cheek spirit of the piece, saluting seriously and playing cowboys and Indians with Sarry with boyish aplomb. He was clearly delighted with his new role, which was extremely exotic to a Russian born in Latvia. Feld said that he rehearsed so intensely that they could not work together for more than an hour and a half at a time: the give and take of ideas and energy, so exciting to the observer, was too exhausting.

Baryshnikov's preoccupation with his new choreographer and other commitments abroad momentarily gave some breathing space to his colleagues at American Ballet Theatre, a deficit-conscious organization that rejoices in his box-office appeal and schedules him for frequent performances whenever he is available. During the company's 1977 winter session in New York, in which Baryshnikov did not participate, danseurs Ivan Nagy, Fernando Bujones, and Ted Kivitt were once again assured of regular performances. At other times, the strain of rivalry has led Bujones to utter such rash statements as "Baryshnikov has the publicity, but I have the talent," which may be understandable, if egotistical, coming from a young man who has just been thrust out of the limelight. Still, there is plenty of time for Bujones to establish himself again as a superstar. He does have an astonishing technique, even if his performing personality still needs to be tempered by maturity.

In the ranks of the Royal Ballet, Baryshnikov, like Nureyev, is still a comparatively rare figure. Dame Ninette de Valois and her successors, Sir Frederick Ashton and Kenneth MacMillan, have adhered consistently to their rule of British dancers for British ballet—though recently the Royal has slipped its guard a bit to allow guest appearances by Baryshnikov and Richard Cragun, among others. This is justified in terms of "bringing the best to the British audience," since a lone superstar is a good deal less expensive to import than a whole company the size of American Ballet Theatre. The Royal is reflecting a current trend in international dance, one that has long been common in opera and in the concert hall.

However, Baryshnikov is not quite the fox-among-hens that Nureyev was when he first pounced on the British ballet scene. Since that time, standards of male dancing in England have risen to such an extent that English-trained danseurs are now ranked among the finest in the world.

Among these outstanding performers is Anthony Dowell. He was at first a reluctant student of ballet, focusing more on the theatrical aspects of dance and on his interest in painting and design (a talent he still pursues as a sometime costume designer); but by his teens he was confirmed in his ambition to dance. He has since become a danseur noble of international stature, one half of a legendary partnership with Antoinette Sibley and at the same time a virtuoso in his own right. His speed, brilliance, and control were first seen when he danced the role of Oberon in Frederick Ashton's *The Dream* (1964), the first ballet to be set on Sibley and Dowell. At the same time, he displayed a cool authority and a classical purity of line that are the marks of the true danseur noble.

From that early beginning emerged a partnership between two individuals whose temperament, musicality, physique, and style are extraordinarily complementary. The two were seen together in all the classics and in Ashton ballets—such as *Daphnis and Chloe, Symphonic Variations,* and *Cinderella*—which, although not created for them, soon seemed peculiarly their own. They were cast together in Robbins's *Afternoon of a Faun* and *Dances at a Gathering;* they matured together as dramatic artists in MacMillan's *Romeo and Juliet,* for which their New York fans in 1974 gave them a twenty-five-minute ovation. That same year, MacMillan choreographed the full-length *Manon* for them.

But Dowell has also danced with other partners and has been seen in a number of works in which he is the lone protagonist. In 1967, Antony Tudor created his first ballet in England since 1939, *Shadowplay,* setting the principal role of The Boy with Matted Hair on Dowell, who considers the experience of working with Tudor on this ballet a turning point in his career, for it taught him to consider the whole ballet and the inner life and meaning of his role. Since then, Dowell's most significant

Anthony Dowell, premier danseur of the Royal Ballet, as Oberon in Sir Frederick Ashton's The Dream. *This was the first major role Dowell created.*

Anthony Dowell and Rudolf Nureyev in Maurice Béjart's *male duet,* Songs of a Wayfarer.

Top: *Sir Frederick Ashton rehearsing Lynn Seymour and Anthony Dowell in his* A Month in the Country, *inspired by Turgenev*. Above: *Dowell and Antoinette Sibley, the great contemporary partnership of British ballet, in Ashton's* Daphnis and Chloe. Opposite: *David Wall as des Grieux (left) and Dowell as Lescaut—an exchange of their usual roles—in MacMillan's* Manon. *Although less known to the international dance public than Dowell, Wall is a mainstay of the Royal Ballet's repertory. He performs a wide range of roles, from the classics to modern works to ballets that call upon his considerable skills as a dancer-actor.*

role creations have been Beliaev in Frederick Ashton's *A Month in the Country* (1976) and the central figure in van Manen's *Four Schumann Pieces* (1975). Of his role in the latter work, London *Times* critic John Percival wrote: ''The qualities which Ashton and Tudor revealed in him, respectively as Oberon and the novice of *Shadowplay,* are combined here: the authority and the introspection, the speed and control, the confidence and reserve.''

Dowell is the preeminent danseur among the Royal's homegrown stars, but he is not the only one—if he were, then his individual genius would have to be credited for his achievements rather than the much improved standards of British male technique. Of the present roster at the Royal Ballet, red-haired David Wall is noted for his *demi-caractère* creation of Lescaut in *Manon.* Dowell, in his newfound dramatic security, has been known to reverse roles with Wall in this ballet, playing Lescaut to Wall's des Grieux, as well as often assuming the part of Mercutio when Wall performs the title role in *Romeo and Juliet.* Wall is also noted for the Ashton pas de deux *The Walk to the Paradise Garden,* which was set for him and Merle Park. He has been a frequent partner of both Fonteyn and Park in the nineteenth-century classics.

Michael Coleman, another star of the Royal, is known for his insouciant Colas in Ashton's *La Fille Mal Gardée,* his mocking Mercutio, and the soaring clarity of his Bluebird. Wayne Eagling is fulfilling the Royal's hopes for him as a future star in such diverse works as *Romeo,* MacMillan's Japanese theater-influenced *Rituals,* and Tetley's *Voluntaries,* recently staged at Covent Garden. His romantic good looks and elegant line also suit him to the traditional danseur noble roles. The small bundle of bounding energy that is Wayne Sleep has proved an inspiration to Ashton on a number of memorable occasions, despite his lack of inches, which would have precluded a career in ballet were he not so strong a dancer technically and so gifted with ballon. In addition to Kolia in Ashton's *A Month in the Country,* Sleep has created a role in the Saturday section of *Jazz Calendar* and George Robertson Sinclair in *Enigma Variations.* MacMillan has choreographed a hilarious pas de deux in his *Elite Syncopations* for Sleep and a much taller girl. As noted previously, Sleep inherits many of the character roles that were the province of the recently retired Alexander Grant. In addition to this list of danseurs—which could easily be extended to include such names as Desmond Kelly, David Ashmole, and Nicholas Johnson—the Royal Ballet has the tradition (which flourishes as well in the Royal Danish Ballet), of dancers such as Michael Somes who are no longer at the peak of their virtuosity and so have taken over character and mime roles, thereby lending weight and authority to the classics and to dramatic ballets.

New York Times critic Clive Barnes has suggested that the Royal Ballet performs better in New York than it does in London, where audiences tend to take their homegrown talent somewhat for granted. He might say the same of America's reaction to its own danseurs: if his name is John Smith, he *can't* be as good as what's's name who just defected. But American-born Richard Cragun has "beaten the system" by both studying and making his career abroad, with Germany's Stuttgart Ballet. He returned in triumph to the United States on the Stuttgart's first American tour, in 1969.

In 1949, Margot Fonteyn and the Royal Ballet conquered the American dance world; twenty years later, the Stuttgart Ballet had a similar impact, in the course of which the company's stellar partnership of prima ballerina Marcia Haydée and Richard Cragun established its international reputation. During the tour, the couple, lovers offstage as well as on, appeared in *The Taming of the Shrew,* a ballet created for their special talents in 1969 by John Cranko, the company's director and choreographer. On the basis of his virile, swashbuckling performance in this ballet, which included the astonishing technical feat of triple *tours en l'air,* Cragun was hailed as a sort of Errol Flynn of the dance. And in contrast to the knockabout pas de deux of this piece, his tender partnering of Haydée in Cranko's *Romeo and Juliet* enhanced his image as a cavalier.

Cragun's emergence as a leading danseur was largely due to the late John Cranko, the man behind the Stuttgart's rise to international prominence. Much of Cranko's choreography was focused on the technical and dramatic abilities of his danseurs, and in Cragun he found a sensitive, versatile instrument for his dance ideas. As part of his strategy to build a company of international stature out of a provincial one, Cranko chose Cragun from the Stuttgart corps de ballet for a number of important roles. In 1965, he created *Opus One* for the danseur, a journey of a soul that is one of his finest choreographies and a ballet most closely associated with Cragun. In 1972, Cragun was one of four friends of the choreographer to be given a movement to dance in *Initials R.B.M.E.,* an affectionate tribute from Cranko to *R*ichard Cragun, German ballerina *B*irgit Keil, *M*arcia Haydée, and another leading danseur of the Stuttgart company, Danish *E*gon Madsen. But in 1973, Cranko died suddenly of a heart attack following one of the company's tremendously successful appearances in the United States. Thus ended tragically the directorship that had fostered the partnership and careers of Haydée and Cragun and had produced such works as *Jeu de Cartes,* a vehicle for the impish elevation of Madsen, and the dramatic *Eugene Onegin,* a ballet most often associated with Haydée and the German danseur Heinz Clauss. The company looked for a new director and a new source of repertoire.

Cranko had been much loved in Stuttgart, and his genius

Opposite: *Wayne Sleep as Kolia in Ashton's dramatic ballet,* A Month in the Country. *Top: Nicholas Johnson as Mercutio, fatally stabbed in the duel with Tybalt, in MacMillan's* Romeo and Juliet. *Above: Wayne Eagling in MacMillan's* Rituals.

for creating story ballets (*Shrew, Onegin, Romeo,* and others) was unique. Yet with the tribute to Cranko, *Voluntaries,* which guest choreographer Glen Tetley produced in 1973 for Haydée, Cragun, Keil, Reid Anderson, and Jan Stripling in the leads, the Stuttgart company felt that it had found a worthy successor, and in 1974 Tetley assumed the directorship.

Like Cranko before him, Tetley utilized Cragun's spectacular gifts in a number of new roles, including an ambitious restaging of *Daphnis and Chloe,* which also featured Madsen as Pan. But Tetley's tenure with the Stuttgart was short-lived. Cranko had produced such varied choreography as the brilliantly modern *Opus One,* the playfully avant-garde *Présence,* and the daringly topical *Traces,* which was concerned with the efforts of a concentration camp survivor (Haydée) to lead a normal life despite crippling memories of her dead husband (Cragun). But his most popular and familiar work—the story ballets and his

reworking of the classics—was firmly rooted in the nineteenth-century classical tradition. Tetley, on the other hand, had evolved a linear, fluid style most notable for its fusion of techniques from both ballet and modern dance. His dances were more esoteric than Cranko's in their choice of music and theme, and they did not cater to the Stuttgart audience, which had only lately been wooed to ballet by Cranko's pragmatic determination to please. But although the experiment failed in Stuttgart, Tetley's ballets—including *Voluntaries* and his orgiastic, male-dominated *The Rite of Spring*—are entering the international repertoire. His work is highly representative of two current trends in the dance world: the mingling of the disciplines of classical and modern dance; and the increasing use of male protagonists, under the influence of modern dance, which, with its traditional emphasis on weight and gravity, is focusing new attention on the performance strengths of the danseur.

Facets of the Stuttgart Ballet. Opposite: *Glen Tetley (right), formerly director of the Stuttgart, rehearses the company's leading dancers, Richard Cragun and Marcia Haydée.* Left: *Egon Madsen as the impish Joker in the late John Cranko's* Jeu de Cartes. Below: *Tetley's* Daphnis and Chloe, *with Cragun and Haydée in the title roles. Tetley's choreography is a fusion of classical and modern techniques.*

Opposite: *Richard Cragun of the Stuttgart Ballet in Kenneth MacMillan's* Requiem. *Right:* Heinz Clauss in the title role and Marcia Haydée as Tatiana, in John Cranko's three-act ballet Eugene Onegin, *first performed by the Stuttgart Ballet in 1965. Below:* Cragun and Haydée in Cranko's version of the full-length Prokofiev Romeo and Juliet.

8

Once-Sacred Boundaries: The "Barefoot Ballet"

One of the most distinctive art forms of America's raw-boned, rough-and-tumble spirit is modern dance, as vigorously American in its origins as jazz—and, like jazz, now universally applauded and performed. In addition to the airborne ballet with its goals of grace and flight, today's danseur must be familiar with a variety of techniques; the most important of these is the "barefoot" form of dance called modern, with its solid, no-nonsense knowledge of ground and gravity.

Once considered the antitheses of each other, ballet and modern dance have been moving together cautiously for several generations, although the danseur who crossed over from one technique to the other was, until recently, relatively rare. Today this practice is becoming commonplace, and the ballet company that includes modern works in its standard repertoire is more the rule than the exception.

Generally speaking, modern dance is based on two principles, which share certain similarities and which both allow a great range of expression. Martha Graham, during the 1920s, developed a technique of "contraction and release," which is derived from the process of breathing; at about the same time, Doris Humphrey evolved her "fall and recovery," which is based on the law of gravity and the individual's balance (or imbalance) in relation to it. Both techniques made it possible to focus on the expressive powers of movement; the result has been a continuing quest to find new ways to evoke meaning through movement. Since the emphasis was on the inherently dramatic powers of the body, a strict story line became unnecessary, even superfluous, and nonliteral abstractions became commonplace. Modern dance is usually performed without shoes—and this is as good a definition of it as many others. Whereas classical ballet has a strictly defined center, from which all movement emanates and to which all movement returns, modern dance concerns itself more with the exploration of movement that is asymmetrical, off-center. Modern dance has never attempted to mask the fact that work is in-volved—in contrast to ballet, which hides all effort beneath its technique. Ballet is usually confined to a specific performing area, such as a stage, whereas modern dance today has consciously sought out new performing spaces, such as gymnasiums, museums, parks, streets, churches, and armories. In its broadest description, modern dance is, as one writer has said, "a form of Western theatrical dancing that has developed almost entirely outside the ballet tradition."

Neither technique is easy to master, and mastering *both* is extremely difficult, because the styles are founded on different principles. Rudolf Nureyev is the most prominent example of a dancer who dared: in 1965, he performed Rudi van Dantzig's *Monument for a Dead Boy,* a ballet as contemporary in its sociological content as in its style. Nureyev's expansion of his technique from ballet to modern was greeted with surprise by the dance world; many reacted as though such a crossover had never been attempted before. To a degree that may have been true—since there are so few danseurs of Nureyev's stature—but the eagerness of male dancers to leap the high fence between the two forms can be documented for several generations of performers. Nureyev, however, was big news, and his decisions carried a substantial weight that began to affect the way other male dancers regarded their art. Having begun his exploration of the modern idiom with van Dantzig, Nureyev went on to make what amounted to a second career, performing a number of other major modern roles, in works by José Limón *(The Moor's Pavane),* Paul Taylor *(Aureole, Big Bertha, The Book of Beasts),* Maurice Béjart *(Songs of a Wayfarer, The Rite of Spring),* Glen Tetley *(Field Figures, Laborintus, Tristan, Pierrot Lunaire),* Murray Louis *(Moment),* and Martha Graham *(Lucifer, The Scarlet Letter, Appalachian Spring,* and *Night Journey).* The scope and variety of these roles are impressive in themselves, but they are also representative of goals shared by leading danseurs today—goals that would have been unthinkable in the realm of ballet a generation or two ago.

Preceding pages: *Ross Parkes (left), Janet Eilber, Tim Wengerd, and Diane Gray of the Martha Graham Dance Company in Graham's* Point of Crossing, *based on the biblical story of Esau and Jacob.* Above: *Lawrence Rhodes (arms outstretched), Dennis Wayne, and members of the now-disbanded Harkness Ballet in* Monument for a Dead Boy, *choreographed by Rudi van Dantzig, artistic director of the Dutch National Ballet. After several years of freelancing with a number of different companies, including the Eliot Feld Ballet and the Pennsylvania Ballet, Rhodes became a member of Dennis Wayne's company,* Dancers. Left: *Leigh Warren in Christopher Bruce's* Black Angels *for Great Britain's Ballet Rambert, a once-classical company that now emphasizes modern dance.*

Two modern works in the repertoire of The Joffrey Ballet. Above: *Paul Sutherland and Lisa Bradley as the doomed young lovers in Alvin Ailey's* Feast of Ashes. *Opposite top:* From The Green Table, *an Expressionistic work by Kurt Jooss, the Diplomats make war at the green table. Opposite bottom: Choreographer Jooss coaches Christian Holder in his own original role of Death.*

When leading danseurs such as Nureyev and, more recently, Baryshnikov express an interest in expanding their range, the selection of ballets in a company repertoire is quite naturally affected. Audiences—no longer prejudiced to the point of excluding one form in favor of another—have come to expect diversity in the programs they see on the ballet stage. And this in turn has helped to broaden the technical base of modern-day ballet companies, as well as the range of works generally offered.

The Royal Ballet, for example, which is generally considered to be the finest classical company in the West, has acquired works by Glen Tetley, Hans van Manen, and younger choreographers working in the same vein. American Ballet Theatre, another company with a foundation in classical technique, has included works by Twyla Tharp, Alvin Ailey, Glen Tetley, and Jerome Robbins—works that may not be strictly "modern" by some definitions, but that use styles of movement that do not qualify them as strictly balletic either. The Royal Ballet and American Ballet Theatre will never be considered modern companies, of course, in the sense that Graham's and Merce Cunningham's companies are, but they strive for an eclecticism that is missing in many modern troupes and that is undoubtedly a factor in the enormous appeal these ballet companies have for ever-increasing audiences.

A rather dramatic and decisive step was taken in 1966 by the London-based Ballet Rambert under the guidance of its director Norman Morrice. The company's technical base was shifted entirely from classical to modern, subsequently taking on a repertoire of works by leading modern choreographers such as Anna Sokolow, Paul Taylor, Louis Falco, Cliff Keuter, Lar Lubovitch, van Dantzig, and Glen Tetley. Tetley is one of the first contemporary dance choreographers to borrow from both modern and classical dance for the creation of ballet; he has fused the angularity and movement modes of modern with the flowing lines of dancers in pointe shoes. As is typical of contemporary choreographers, Tetley's experience is diverse: he trained with the modern dancers Hanya Holm, Margaret Craske, and Martha Graham and studied ballet with Antony Tudor. His career has been made mostly in Europe, where his theatrical blend of styles has found a large and appreciative audience, and he has choreographed for a number of leading companies, including the Royal Ballet, the Netherlands Dance Theater, and the Royal Danish Ballet. Most recently, he was director of the Stuttgart Ballet.

Tetley was one of the first people sought out by Norman Morrice at the time of Rambert's change. The company's first "new-wave" ballet, choreographed by Tetley, was *Ziggurat.* "It changed our ideas about setting," Morrice has written, "about lighting, about the shape of choreography and music.

For us it was a totally new experience, and although working with him was extremely demanding, it certainly helped to increase our stamina.''

The Dutch National Ballet is another company with a reputation for its productions of the standard classics. But under the directorship of Hans van Manen, Rudi van Dantzig, and Toer van Schayk, it has developed an image all its own. Van Dantzig's training is as eclectic as Tetley's: he began in ballet, but by the time he had begun to choreograph as well as dance, he had fallen under the influence of Martha Graham. Something of his character has permeated the company, and it is with them that Nureyev first danced his role in van Dantzig's *Monument for a Dead Boy.*

Other companies that have moved in the same direction include the Stuttgart Ballet, particularly when it was under the direction of Glen Tetley; the Royal Danish Ballet, whose director-choreographer has made considerable headway in revamping the classics and introducing new works by such modern choreographers as Paul Taylor and Murray Louis; and the Batsheva Dance Company, an Israeli modern dance company that has been fused with a ballet company.

In every ballet company the director's taste is a dominant factor in the selection of a repertoire. Robert Joffrey, for example, is constantly searching for new works and old—particularly ballets from the Diaghilev era—to set on his company. Perhaps the most interesting acquisitions the company has made in this

Above: *Russell Sultzbach as Icarus and Ted Nelson as Daedalus in Gerald Arpino's* The Relativity of Icarus. Left: *Ted Shawn in his* Invocation to the Thunderbird. Opposite: *Erick Hawkins in his modern* Here and Now with Watchers.

area have been the works of the modern dance choreographer Kurt Jooss. In 1967, The Joffrey added the first of its several Jooss ballets to the repertoire, *The Green Table*.

Jooss's modern masterpiece in the Expressionist style was choreographed in Germany in 1932. The subject of the work is war, and the theme is man's inability to avoid it. Coming when it did, at the onset of the Nazi determination to conquer Western Europe, its theme was topical in its day; with time and perspective, however, the work has proved itself to be universal. Most modern ballets from the years of experimentation and social content do not wear well in revival; *The Green Table* is a notable exception.

Jooss's concept for the central figure of the ballet, Death, was based on his idea of a medieval dance of death; the character personifying Death sweeps and stamps his way inexorably through a population beset by the brutal waste of war. Like so many of the early moderns, Jooss sought his movement in sources outside ballet: he derived the dominant motif for Death's dance, for instance, from his experiences working on a farm with a scythe as a young man. Jooss choreographed Death for himself, tailoring the movement to his own talents as a dancer. This is one example of the tendency of modern choreographers to create roles suited to their own idiomatic style; it has often been a stumbling block in reconstructing a work years later, since the demands are so individual that it is difficult —if not impossible—to capture the essential ingredients of a performance once its creator has stopped dancing the role. However, the effectiveness of the dramatic choreography, coupled with a powerful performance, makes *The Green Table* one of the masterpieces of modern dance.

Death was one of the few roles created for the male performer during a period of modern dance history—the 1930s— when the field was dominated by women choreographers performing female roles. *The Green Table* also contains important

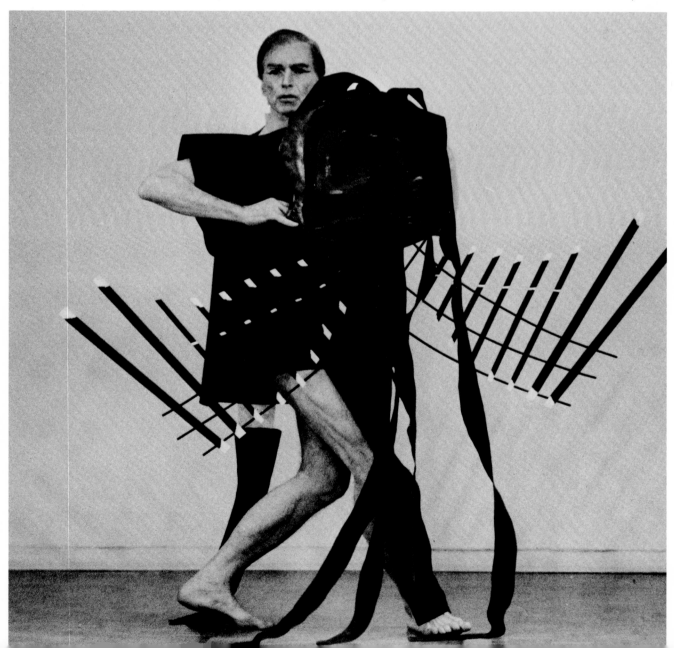

vignettes for male dancers in such roles as soldiers, diplomats, a Standard Bearer, and an unctuous Profiteer, for whom Jooss created undulating, sinuous movement and even borrowed a bit from the con man's sleight-of-hand routines.

The Joffrey Ballet's leading contemporary choreographer is Gerald Arpino, whose output over the years can hardly be rivaled for range in style and experimentation. He has created ballets such as *Kettentanz, Viva Vivaldi!,* and *Reflections,* which rely on classical technique, and *Sea Shadow,* which combines disciplines in a romantic pas de deux, in which the ballerina dances on pointe in an expression of idealized love and the danseur performs barefoot, as a statement about the nature of earthly passion. Working in another vein, Arpino combined theatrics with sociology in such modern ballets as *The Clowns, Sacred Grove on Mount Tamalpais,* and *Trinity,* in the last of which the dancers' upraised fists represent the rebellion of youth. And he has drawn on modern dance techniques in conjunction with athletics and the lyrical lines of ballet in such works as *Olympics* (an all-male ballet), the comic *Valentine,* and a projected trilogy based on mythological themes that includes *The Relativity of Icarus* and *Orpheus Times Light*[2], both of which feature male protagonists.

Arpino champions the cause of the male dancer, and his ballets have featured such danseurs as Paul Sutherland, Chris-

tian Holder, Dermot Burke, Gary Chryst, Dennis Wayne, and Russell Sultzbach—representatives of a whole new generation of young dancers with classical training who are expected to be conversant with a variety of dance styles—including modern dance.

The early leaders of the modern movement were all women who declared their independence as human beings and as artists. This freedom is important in considering their contributions, because it became one of the cornerstones of the modern canon. Loie Fuller, Isadora Duncan, Ruth St. Denis, and Mary Wigman—the first three Americans and the fourth a German—were each vastly different from one another in terms of the style and content of their dances, but as forerunners of modern dance they broke the spiritual ground that gave rise to modern dancers such as Martha Graham, Doris Humphrey, Charles Weidman, Hanya Holm, Kurt Jooss, Harald Kreutzberg.

Ted Shawn, a dancer in his own right who married Ruth St. Denis in 1914, began his proselytizing for the rights of men to dance in America long before the subject was even an issue, much less a possibility. At the turn of the century, men simply did not perform "serious" dance on stage in America—it was regarded as unmanly, and it allowed no possibility for making a living. With St. Denis, Shawn formed a company and a school

Below: *Martha Graham (seated near mirror) during rehearsal of the men in her* Lucifer, *a work created for Nureyev and Fonteyn.* Right: *Nureyev as the Moor and Louis Falco as the Moor's Friend in* The Moor's Pavane, *a work by José Limón based on Shakespeare's* Othello. *Limón, a distinguished modern dancer, directed his own company for twenty-five years until his death in 1972;* The Moor's Pavane *has also been performed by many other companies. Falco danced with Limón and now directs his own modern dance troupe; he has also choreographed works for Netherlands Dance Theater and Ballet Rambert.* Bottom left: *Nureyev in* Lucifer. Bottom right: *Bertram Ross and Ethel Winter in Graham's* Night Journey.

called Denishawn, which was a major influence on the development of dance in the United States—about the only influence, in fact, for a number of years. Shawn stoutly resisted the prejudice of the times and must be given credit for holding the Denishawn enterprises together for as long as he did—until he and St. Denis parted company in 1931. Two years later, the determined Shawn formed his famous all-male dance company, calling it Ted Shawn and His Men Dancers. The emphasis was on a form of dance that borrowed its technique from athletics and "manly" activities; traveling the country on arduous tours of one-night stands in any town that would have them, Shawn's dancers did a great deal in their seven years as a company toward clearing the way for other men to enter the field. Based on a farm in Massachusetts, which came to be known as Jacob's Pillow, the men led an active and much-publicized Spartan existence, building their own lodgings, clearing their own land, raising their own food, and so on. Shawn's company lasted until the Second World War, when a number of its leading dancers were drafted into the army. During the ensuing years, Jacob's Pillow became the nation's first great summer dance festival devoted to all forms of dance—ethnic, jazz, ballet, modern—and helped to unite the various forms in the midst of a growing dance audience.

Martha Graham, a student of Shawn's and later a performer with Denishawn, left Denishawn in 1923; Doris Humphrey and Charles Weidman followed suit in 1928. Graham became the dominant figure in modern dance, as well as a major artistic force in the twentieth century. Her early strident attacks against ballet were aimed at the rather vapid works produced during the early years of this century; and the schism created between ballet and modern dance was not officially healed until Graham herself announced in 1974 that the war "against frivolity" was over.

In Europe, Kreutzberg, Jooss, and Wigman eventually ran into the insurmountable barriers presented by the Second World War, which brought the development of modern dance to a halt there. In America, where the road to a dance career for men had been bulldozed open by the efforts of Ted Shawn, we experienced the impact of a new eclecticism in dance. Graham, for example, entered into an interesting early experiment with the choreographer Léonide Massine. In his 1930 staging of The Rite of Spring, the first performance of this work in the United States, Graham devised her own solo for the central role of the Chosen Virgin, while Massine, with his balletic base, choreographed the rest of the ballet. The collaboration marks an early attempt to find a common ground between ballet and modern—a search that increased in intensity as the years passed.

American themes proliferated in dance (and theater) during the period of nationalism that culminated with the war in the 1940s, resulting in ballets such as Lew Christensen's Filling Station and Eugene Loring's Billy the Kid. First performed in 1938, both works contained strong central roles for male dancers—Christensen and Loring created these roles for themselves—and used a wider range of movement than had been possible previously. Eliot Carter's Pocahontas was another work by a young choreographer, and it featured in a leading role the ballet-trained dancer Erick Hawkins, who was to become one of the first dancers to switch to the modern style exclusively.

With the early exceptions in America of Charles Weidman and Ted Shawn, very few men could be found in modern dance in the 1920s and 1930s. Graham's dances, until the late 1930s, were all for women. Her technique had been designed to express intense passion; but in the early dances this passion was not sexual. Graham explored social themes, contemporary ideas, prevailing psychology; but not until 1938 did men begin to take on importance in her works. That year the first male dancer appeared with her company: Erick Hawkins, refugee from Ballet Caravan and destined to be—for a short while—Graham's husband. Hawkins stayed with the company until 1951, during which time a number of important roles in the Graham repertoire were created for him: the Lover in Letter to the World (1940), the Dark Beloved in Deaths and Entrances (1943), the Husbandman in Appalachian Spring (1944), and He Who Summons in Dark Meadow (1946).

After leaving Graham, Hawkins formed his own company, which—in the manner of most modern companies—performed exclusively his own distinctive style of dance; in Hawkins's case this was based on an intense intellectualization of movement, a trend that was followed by Graham's second male dancer, Merce Cunningham. Cunningham was with Graham from 1939 to 1945, and his own experimentation eventually changed American perceptions of modern dance as dramatically as Graham's had. Other male dancers for whom Graham created roles and who went on to become leaders of the modern dance movement were John Butler, whose work included choreography for television and opera; Robert Cohan, who directed the London Contemporary Dance Theatre, which today has a strong range of roles for men; Paul Taylor, who became a prominent innovator in his own right; Bertram Ross, one of Graham's principal dancers for twenty-five years; Ross Parkes, well known as a soloist with a number of leading modern companies; and Tim Wengerd, currently at the top of the Graham roster as a leading male dancer.

Graham's choreography after 1938 contained substantial roles for men, although the female dancer remained a dominant personality in her dances until after she had herself retired from the stage. The situation was altered in the early 1970s with her

Merce Cunningham (right) with Susanah Haymen-Chaffey and Charles Moulton in Cunningham's Signals. *A foremost modern dancer and choreographer, Cunningham was a member of Martha Graham's company during the 1940s; since 1952 he has directed and danced with his own company, frequently setting his works for them to the music of avant-garde composers.*

creation of ballets such as *Lucifer, The Scarlet Letter,* and *Point of Crossing.* Clive Barnes, the dance critic for the *New York Times,* suggests that Rudolf Nureyev, dancing in the first two of these works, helped to restore to Graham's company some of the pioneering spirit that had characterized its earlier days. True, Nureyev's ballet technique tended to surface while performing these distinctly nonballetic roles—his tendency to seek a balance or to round and soften an angular line has often been noted by Graham purists; nevertheless, the danseur provided new blood, a salty and stimulating presence that revealed itself in performance. The Graham company today boasts a particularly able contingent of male dancers who fill a repertoire that is still expanding.

In 1959, Graham collaborated with George Balanchine in a ballet called *Episodes,* which was based on an interchange of techniques and dancers. For this gesture of friendship between the two art forms, Graham choreographed the first section for herself and ballerina Sallie Wilson, and Balanchine set the solo in his second section on a young dancer in Graham's company named Paul Taylor. Taylor was a sensation. Lincoln Kirstein described his dancing as "A prolonged acrobatic motor sequence of anguished sound strung on negative gesture ranging from purr to scratch or buzz to strangle." And Taylor's performance was a "long preface of madly tortured, whimsically anxious, captiously awkward movement." The event resulted in a deluge of requests from other male modern dancers for Balanchine to create similar vehicles to extend their techniques—requests that were not fulfilled. In fact, Taylor's solo was never set on any other dancer and is now lost.

One of the tenets of modern dance is its freedom from the academic strictures of ballet; this same freedom also encourages experimentation. As a result, a number of modern companies have formed over the the years, most of them taking the names of their principal choreographer and dancer.

The most successful dancer to break away from the company formed by Doris Humphrey and Charles Weidman was the Mexican-born José Limón, whose works are filled with a feeling for ritual and tradition—strongly dramatic, possessed by overwhelming passion, primitive. A large man, Limón's dances tend toward expansive gestures that betray a feeling too deep for words. The modern dance preference for isolating critically dramatic situations and recreating their essence through dance is most successfully attained in Limón's masterpiece, *The Moor's Pavane,* which takes its themes of jealousy and deception from Shakespeare's *Othello.* Set to court dances by the seventeenth-century composer Henry Purcell, the title role of the Moor was first danced by Limón himself. The work's tensions are derived from the tautly contained, formalized decorum of the dancers' pavane—the central image of restraint—

which builds to an explosive conclusion. The work is now in the repertoire of a number of ballet companies, including American Ballet Theatre, the Royal Danish Ballet, the Royal Swedish Ballet, the National Ballet of Canada, and The Joffrey Ballet. The last dancer with whom Limón worked on the Moor before his death in 1972 was Rudolf Nureyev, who now includes the work in his concert repertoire.

There are a number of interesting reasons why men have found themselves drawn to the realm of modern dance. One is the added challenge offered by an art form that encourages a wide range of expression. In ballet, the dancer must begin training when he is very young, which requires forming a clear-cut professional goal at an age when few of us know what we are going to do with our lives. By contrast, there is greater flexibility in modern dance, and many leading figures have approached the field with a professional goal in mind only after they have become adults, well past the age when ballet training could be profitably begun. Glen Tetley was in medical school before he began his studies with Hanya Holm; Paul Taylor was on scholarship studying painting before he decided to go to The Juilliard School to study dance; and even Ted Shawn, who would proselytize so effectively for the dignity of the professional male dancer, was an adult headed for a career in the ministry before he decided to change the direction of his life. Such examples in modern dance are numerous.

Another factor in making modern dance an attractive field for men is that it permits a somewhat longer performing career than is possible in ballet. While a ballet dancer is usually set out to pasture by the time he reaches his late thirties or early forties, men in modern dance seem to keep going into their fifties and beyond. Ted Shawn was one of these; Charles Weidman, who performed with his company when he was over seventy, was another; Erick Hawkins, now in his sixties, is still performing regularly; and Merce Cunningham, in his fifties, seems nowhere near retirement.

Cunningham developed a style that was quite different from Graham's; where she used movement as part of a larger landscape that included decor and a musical score, in his dances these elements are often independent of each other. The style he developed seemed almost balletic, lyrical in feeling. Cunningham inspired a number of followers, including Paul Taylor, who took the balletic elements in modern dance one step further.

Taylor's work ranges from a lyricism that was once unusual for modern dance to the convolutions and angularity of modern angst; his work is appealing to dancers with ballet training because of its obvious extensions of balletic technique, with which Taylor is thoroughly familiar. Nureyev has danced Taylor's own role in his ballet *Aureole,* and has also essayed Taylor's *Book of Beasts,* which he performed with Taylor's company for several seasons. Taylor's *Big Bertha* is a cynical statement on

Opposite: *Paul Taylor rehearsing Nureyev in his own* Aureole.
Above left: *Baryshnikov and Twyla Tharp in her* Once More, Frank. Above: *Baryshnikov in Tharp's* Push Comes to Shove.

181

man's mechanized society; Nureyev has performed in this piece on television, taking the role of the Father, who becomes dehumanized under the influence of a mechanical monster. Like most of Taylor's work, it contains a rather bitter wit that arises from recognizable—and not always very nice—observations about humanity.

During the 1960s, a group of young choreographers based at New York's Judson Memorial Church challenged the conventionally established roles of men and women in dance; in many of their new works, they made these roles interchangeable, giving men and women the same material to perform, and making no distinctions between male and female characterizations. This was a further assault on the sexual barriers thrown up by society in general and by dance in particular; both men and women were to benefit from the new possibilities.

Another person working in the same direction was Twyla Tharp, a former dancer with Paul Taylor's company and one of the most original modern American choreographers. Tharp heads her own company, which consisted solely of women until as late as 1972; when she did take on a male dancer, she gave him roles based on his qualities as a person, not particularly as a man. One of the most notable of these roles is that performed by Mikhail Baryshnikov in Tharp's *Push Comes to Shove* (1976). Even Tharp's costumes have a slightly asexual feeling to them, often being the same for both men and women.

Modern dance also provided an early home for black dancers at a time when, mistakenly, it was believed that blacks had no place in ballet. Arthur Mitchell was to prove this position wrong; but before he did, other black men—including Alvin Ailey and Louis Johnson—took advantage of the greater hospitality to make a career in dance and enrich modern dance with their choreographic gifts.

The dancers in Alvin Ailey's City Center Dance Theater, a troupe best known for its striking theatricality and infectious energy, perform in a variety of styles—jazz, African, calypso, ballet, modern. Ailey is one of the first modern choreographers to mix dance styles, which he began doing in the 1950s; he is also one of the first choreographers whose works have appealed to a broad audience untutored in either ballet or modern. Ailey has achieved the goal of making his company a repository for the best modern works of the recent past (especially works by Lester Horton and black choreographers such as Talley Beatty and Louis Johnson), as well as a place to show his own enormously popular dances. Among the revivals he has presented is Ted Shawn's *Kinetic Molpai,* originally choreographed in 1935 for nine of Shawn's Men Dancers and re-created for Ailey by Barton Mumaw, a dancer from Shawn's original men's troupe. One of the leading male dancers with

Ailey is the charismatic Dudley Williams, who is seen to his best advantage in such Ailey works as *Revelations,* where he performs the "I Want To Be Ready" solo; *Blues Suite,* in the Chicago dance hall scene; and *Love Songs,* created for Williams and Judith Jamison in 1972—all works that reveal Williams's flowing musical style, magnetism, and stage presence.

Not until Ailey was in college in the early 1950s did he decide, under the influence of the West Coast dancer and choreographer Lester Horton, to go into modern dance. Indian, black, Oriental—from the beginning his training and taste was eclectic. After the Horton company disbanded, Ailey moved East and performed for a while as an actor and dancer off-Broadway while studying with the modern dancers Graham, Humphrey, Holm, and Weidman (to whom his later pantomimic style in dance owes a great debt), as well as Jane Dudley and Karel Shook. His early all-black dance companies set out to show what black art could be—not the least of which was the possibility of a respectable career for black men in serious modern dance. Today, welcoming dancers of all cultures, Ailey's company is a perennial favorite on the New York and touring scenes.

Although Maurice Béjart's company is, strictly speaking, a ballet company, it also has many of the elements that draw dance—modern and ballet—ever closer to the theater. Béjart's choreography is distinctive, based on balletic technique, but expanded to include Oriental, modern, folk dancing, Indian, even discotheque—any kind of movement that might be a means to the ends of Béjart's eclectic choreography. In recent years, Béjart has tailored these highly theatrical works to the talents of two ballet-trained danseurs of unusual talent: Paolo Bortoluzzi and Jorge Donn, for whom Béjart has created some of his most technically intricate roles—such as Nijinsky in *Nijinsky, Clown of God* (Donn) or the solo *Nomos Alpha* for Bortoluzzi. Béjart's company regularly features male dancers who are powerful and eloquent, who are poets as well as athletes, and consequently the company's look is distinctly masculine and theatrical.

Béjart's *Firebird* uses the Stravinsky score but discards the Russian fairy tale that originally served as libretto. In Béjart's male-oriented version, the title character is not a ballerina, but the male leader of an underground group fighting the Nazis during the Occupation of France in the Second World War. The leader must be sacrificed; and choreography for this role (which has been danced by Donn and Nureyev, among others) is filled with the anguish and introspection that must belong to a man condemned to die a heroic death. Béjart's *Romeo and Juliet* emphasizes Shakespeare's theme in a contemporary idiom: make love, not war; and his version of *The Rite of Spring,*

Top: *Ailey's production of McKayle's* Rainbow 'Round My Shoulder, *with Dudley Williams (held by Hector Mercado). Above, left to right: Clive Thompson in Ailey's* Revelations; *finale of* Revelations; *Baryshnikov and Judith Jamison in Ailey's* Pas de Duke.

choreographed for a corps of youthful male dancers, is filled with a primitive, propulsive energy that is overtly sexual. *The Ninth Symphony* (set to music by Beethoven) is an example of Béjart's preference for enormous, epic "ballets" that are sweeping in theatrical scope and technically demanding, for a corps that consists of hundreds of dancers.

Béjart's school, Mudra, in Brussels, is oriented toward fashioning total performers, not only dancers, and it develops technical proficiency in singing and acting as well as in dancing. In a historic collaboration with the Comédie Française in 1976, Béjart created *Molière Imaginaire,* a dance-theater work that combined Béjart's Ballet of the Twentieth Century with the acting company from his own school and the illustrious Comédie troupe. Jorge Donn danced and acted the role of Louis XIV and Jan Nuyts was Tartuffe. This was the first time in its long history that the Comédie had allowed guest stars, ballet, or a foreign company to appear on its stage. The collaboration brought dance into even closer association with its near-neighbor and ancestor, theater.

The history of dance and the danseur are now coming full circle. The broad-based entertainments in European courts, which featured acting, pageantry, pomp, and politics as well as dance, gradually drifted toward the esoteric art form of the late nineteenth century appreciated solely by the cognoscenti. Now, under the influence of myriad forms of dance and theater, dance has shifted back and become part of a free-swinging, innovative, broad-based entertainment. In this, the role of the male dancer has been closely linked with the reigning fashion of the times. As founders of ballet, men dominated the stage until strong prejudice diminished their position as performers, nearly to extinction. With the blossoming of intellectual and artistic freedom during the twentieth century, struggles by a handful of pioneers have resulted in the restoration of dignity for men in dance, giving ballet an ever-increasing resource for future endeavors.

The arts have always been a pulse on society: a book tells something about the culture in which it was written; painting reveals perception; dancing, in which it is possible to combine all the arts, gives a rich source of information about ourselves. That men are now free to pursue careers where they were once forbidden is a heartening prognosis for the future of all the arts, as well as for the development of our civilization. In this century, we have observed the development of male dance in such unique individuals as Nijinsky and Fokine, Balanchine and Béjart, all of whom helped spearhead a movement in the history of dance. It may not be as easily defined as the ballerina's rise on to her toes and the subsequent ascendancy of Romantic ballet—but, cumulatively, this movement is a significant symbol of our times: the new, major role of the danseur.

In contrast to George Balanchine, choreographer Maurice Béjart has said, "Ballet is man." Danseurs Paolo Bortoluzzi and Jorge Donn have often appeared as the protagonists in his ballets. Opposite top: *Bortoluzzi and Nureyev in Béjart's* Songs of a Wayfarer, *a duet created for them in 1971.* Opposite bottom: *Donn in Béjart's* Firebird, *with men from the Ballet of the Twentieth Century.* Above: *Bortoluzzi in Béjart's* Bhakti.

185

Index

Acknowledgments

We do not have sufficient space here to do justice to our long list of source material, but we would like to acknowledge our enormous debt to the splendid research facilities of the Dance Collection of the New York Public Library at Lincoln Center, Library and Museum of the Performing Arts. We would also like to thank Mrs. Mary Whitney, Eleanor Maiella, Margaret Conan, Kathryn Dobrowolski, and Juliana Wu for their help with research; Leslie E. Spatt for her kindness in supplying some of our visual material; our editors, Mimi Koren and Jay Hyams, for their support and assistance in the preparation of the manuscript; and art director Allan Mogel for his superb design of the book.

Photo Credits

The following abbreviations are used:

CGA The Covent Garden Archives, The Royal Opera House, London

DCol Dance Collection, The New York Public Library at Lincoln Center, Library and Museum of the Performing Arts (photos copied by Michael Lawrence)

TM Courtesy of The Theatre Museum, London

MA Mira

AC Anthony Crickmay

FF Fred Fehl

BG Beverly Gallegos

LG Lois Greenfield

EG Edward Griffiths

HK Hannes Killian

DM Dina Makarova

HM Herbert Migdoll

LS Leslie E. Spatt

MS Martha Swope

LDV L. D. Vartoogian

RW Rosemary Winckley

PAGES 1, 4–5 AC 6–7 © John R. Johnsen, 8 MS

Chapter 1

10–11 HM 13 EG 14 LEFT DM, RIGHT LDV 15 LEFT HM, courtesy of WNET, "Dance in America" series RIGHT © HK 16 TOP RW BOTTOM LEFT HM, BOTTOM RIGHT FF 17, 18 © HK 19 LEFT HM, TOP RIGHT FF, BOTTOM RIGHT © HK 20 DCol 21 AC

Chapter 2

22–23 AC 25 TOP LEFT Bibliothèque de l'Institut, DCol, TOP RIGHT © Louis Peres, BOTTOM FF 26 Jennie Walton 27 LS 28 © Houston Rogers 28–29 TOP HM, BOTTOM FF 30 RW 31 BG 32 TOP LEFT EG, BOTTOM LEFT FF, TOP RIGHT BG, BOTTOM RIGHT © Houston Rogers 34 HM 35 TOP LEFT DM, TOP RIGHT © Louis Peres, BOTTOM EG 36 TOP FF, BOTTOM AND 37 BG 39 TOP DM, BOTTOM LEFT © HK, BOTTOM RIGHT FF 41 AC 42 LEFT LS, RIGHT AND 43, 46–47 BG 49 AC

Chapter 3

50, 51, 53, 54 TOP LEFT DCol 54 TOP RIGHT AC, BOTTOM MA 56–57, 59 DCol 60 TOP HM, BOTTOM BG 61 TOP LEFT DCol, TOP RIGHT © LS, BOTTOM LEFT Reg Wilson, BOTTOM RIGHT HM 62 LS 63 DCol 64 TOP HM, BOTTOM AND 65, 66, 67 DCol 68 HM 69 LDV 70–71 Jack Vartoogian

Chapter 4

72–73 HM 75 DCol, 76 HM 77 HM, courtesy of WNET, "Dance in America" series 78 FF 79 Sasha (Radio Times Hulton Picture Library), TM 80 TOP DCol, BOTTOM FF 81, 82, 83 MS 85 George Platt Lynes, DCol 87 TOP FF, BOTTOM LEFT AND RIGHT courtesy of Robert Joffrey (photographer unknown) 88 FF, courtesy of Robert Joffrey 89 FF 90, 91 HM 92 TOP MS, BOTTOM FF 93 TOP FF, BOTTOM George Platt Lynes, DCol 94 TOP AND CENTER FF, BOTTOM Gordon Anthony, TM 95 BG 96 TOP CGA, BOTTOM Baron (Radio Times Hulton Picture Library), TM 97 TOP RIGHT TM, TOP LEFT © Houston Rogers, BOTTOM AC

Chapter 5

98–99 EG 101, 102 AC 103 TOP LEFT MA, TOP RIGHT collection of EG, BOTTOM LDV 104, 105 BG 106–107 MA 107 DM 109 TOP EG, BOTTOM LEFT DM, BOTTOM RIGHT Artkino, DCol, courtesy of Rosa Madell Film Library 110 TOP MA, BOTTOM Jennie Walton 112 © Houston Rogers 113 Jennie Walton 114 EG 115 TOP LEFT RW, TOP RIGHT, BOTTOM LEFT AND RIGHT EG 117 Jennie Walton

Chapter 6

118–119 LDV 121 TOP LEFT FF, TOP RIGHT LDV, BOTTOM CGA 122 TOP LEFT, BOTTOM LEFT © Houston Rogers TOP RIGHT, BOTTOM RIGHT AC 124–125 LDV 125 EG 127, 128 AC 129 EG 130, 131 TOP MS 131 BOTTOM, 132 TOP LDV 132 BOTTOM Jack Vartoogian

Chapter 7

134–135 HM courtesy of WNET, "Dance in America" series 137 FF 139 TOP LEFT DM, TOP RIGHT HM BOTTOM © Mydtskov 140, 141 HM 142–143, 142 BOTTOM MS 143 BOTTOM HM 144 TOP LEFT FF, TOP RIGHT AND BOTTOM HM 145 MS 146–147 HM 147 TOP RW, BOTTOM LEFT HM, BOTTOM RIGHT FF 148 TOP LEFT Jack Vartoogian, TOP RIGHT LG, BOTTOM LEFT MS, BOTTOM RIGHT AND 149 HM 151 TOP RW, BOTTOM DM 152, 153 HM 154, 156–157, 158 TOP AC BOTTOM Alan Cunliffe 159 BG 160, 161, 162 AC 163 © HK 164 © LS 165 © HK

Chapter 8

166–167 MS 169 TOP FF, BOTTOM AC 170 Lewis Brown 171 HM, courtesy of WNET, "Dance in America" series 172 TOP HM, BOTTOM John Lindquist 173 LG 174–175, 174 BOTTOM LEFT AC, BOTTOM RIGHT HM 176 TOP LEFT MS, TOP RIGHT LDV, BOTTOM LEFT MS, BOTTOM RIGHT FF 178–179, 180, 181 LG 183 HM 184 TOP BG, BOTTOM DM 185 RW.